# RELIGION AND REASON JOINED

*"Passion and prejudice govern the world, only under the name of reason. It is our part, by religion and reason joined, to counteract them all we can."*

—John Wesley, letter to John Benson

# RELIGION AND REASON JOINED
## CANDLER AT ONE HUNDRED

CANDLER SCHOOL OF THEOLOGY

By Gary S. Hauk, PhD

Dobbs Hall, still in use at Emory, housed theology students when it opened in 1916.

# RELIGION AND REASON JOINED
## CANDLER AT ONE HUNDRED

ISBN 978-0-692-22472-4

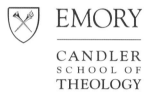

EMORY
CANDLER
SCHOOL OF
THEOLOGY

Candler School of Theology at Emory University
1531 Dickey Dr., Atlanta, GA 30322
Phone: (404) 727-6324
www.candler.emory.edu

Gary S. Hauk, PhD
Author

Copyediting
Sally Wolff King and Bob Land

Project Manager
Renée Peyton

Design
Rick Korab

Indexing
Bob Land

Book Development
Bookhouse Group, Inc.
www.bookhouse.net
Covington, Georgia

By 1922 the campus of Emory University in the Druid Hills section of Atlanta had lost little of its expansive woodlands. The Theology Building is shown at left.

*The Theology Building, 1973.*

# CONTENTS

When the Candler School of Theology began life in September 1914, history had begun to turn on a hinge. It was an altogether splendid time to start a school of theology. It has been an altogether agonizing century in need of ministry.

The history of Candler—so far—is in some ways the history of the twentieth century. Candler began its life the month after "the guns of August" boomed the start of "the war to end all wars." The school was shaped by important currents of liberal theology, and the criticisms of that theology levied from opposite ends of the theological spectrum. Candler's graduates before World War II included a Japanese minister whose church was destroyed in the Hiroshima bombing and who survived to devote his life to nuclear disarmament. Candler grew to maturity during the American civil rights era and played a role in the dismantling of segregation both in the cradle of civil rights—Atlanta—and in Emory University itself. The theology school weathered controversy over "the death of God" during the 1960s while helping to give birth to one of the most eminent graduate programs in religious studies in the world. The library of the school has grown to become the preeminent theology library in the Southeast, perhaps in the nation. When Baylor University in 1996 identified the "twelve most effective preachers" in the English-speaking world, four of them would turn out to have some connection to Candler. For someone interested in the history of theology and theological education, it would be difficult to find anything more engaging than this story.

Yet the Candler School of Theology might not have been born but for the scheming aspiration of a Vanderbilt University chancellor, the godless secularism of a robber baron turned philanthropist, and the recalcitrance of a bunch of Methodist bishops. All of these things made for active ingredients in a lawsuit cooked up for the delectation of the Supreme Court of the state of Tennessee. From the perspective of a century later, it is astonishing how quickly things moved once the table was set. The Tennessee court digested the full course of the lawsuit and rendered its verdict in March 1914; the Methodist Episcopal Church, South—dyspeptic over the court's decision in favor of Vanderbilt— took the first steps to establish a new university in May; Asa Candler, the founder of The Coca-Cola Company, offered a million dollars toward the new university in July; and the new school of theology opened its doors to students on September 23. Along the way, a chancellor of the new university was appointed, the first faculty members were hired, and a new curriculum was laid out.

Elsewhere in the world, other matters were quickly defining the new century. The second decade of the twentieth century was a period of great ferment. In the view of some historians, the 1910s marked the twilight of lingering Victorian sentiment and morality and ushered in the true end of the nineteenth century. In June 1914 Archduke Franz Ferdinand, heir to the throne of Austria-Hungary, was assassinated in Sarajevo, and by the end of the summer all of Europe was at war. Closer to home, the U.S. South was settling into the grip of Jim Crow laws and preparing to fight culturally and legally for old ways of thinking. The Scopes trial in Dayton, Tennessee, was just a decade away and would pit Fundamentalism against the teaching of evolution.

The year after the Methodist Episcopal Church, South, severed its ties with Vanderbilt, a new Methodist university received its charter, and on January 25, 1915, Emory University became home to the Candler School of Theology as well as several other professional schools and the old Emory College. But 1915 also witnessed the infamous lynching of Leo Frank, an innocent man charged with a brutal murder and taken from his jail cell in Marietta, Georgia, to be hanged—probably as much because he was a Jew as for the crime he did not commit. Several months later, in November, the Ku Klux Klan was reborn during a bonfire-heated rally atop Stone Mountain. It was an altogether splendid time to start a school of theology.

Trying to tell this story well in a relatively short space has brought great enjoyment but also challenges. Coming to Emory in 1983 to pursue a doctorate in Christian ethics in the Graduate Division of Religion, I developed close relationships with many of the Candler faculty and have been associated in some ways with the school for three of its ten decades. For me the length of this friendship with Candler is a source of both astonishment (thirty years!) and delight (thirty years!). This friendship also brings a daunting sense of responsibility. Knowing firsthand many of the intricacies of the life of the institution, I find it challenging to draw certain lines. How to separate all the story that must be told from all the story that could be told? How to write a history that both celebrates Candler's first century and fairly unveils the school's missteps and lost opportunities? How to do justice to the contributions of so many men and women who labored in the quieter corners of the vineyard but nevertheless mattered decisively? Inevitably some of my choices will be unsatisfying to some who read this book, and for that I beg forgiveness.

The book had its genesis, of course, in the looming centennial of the school, which prompted Dean Jan Love to ask me in 2010 to think about taking on this project. I am deeply grateful to her for that invitation and the confidence behind it. No less critical was the funding she provided for summer research assistants, digital-image copying, and editorial review.

Pearl Young undertook important preliminary research into the early relationships between Emory and Atlanta, and into the early years of women's enrollment in Candler. Sally Wolff King copyedited the entire manuscript before it went off to the publisher.

Current and emeritus members of the Candler faculty kindly set aside hours to let me interview them: Roberta Bondi, Brooks Holifield, Steve Kraftchick, William Mallard, Max Miller, Carol Newsom, David Pacini, Russ Richey, Don Saliers, Luther Smith, and Jim Waits. Some have kindly read earlier versions of chapters and offered helpful suggestions to improve them: Pat Graham and Steve Kraftchick. Brooks Holifield read the entire first draft of the manuscript and pushed me to pay more attention to the currents and eddies of theological developments in the school. To the extent that I have satisfied his wished-for history of ideas, the book is better. To the extent that I have not, I hope that I have at least suggested some of the richness of the commitment to intellectual life at Candler and have paved the way for another writer to do more in this arena.

The superbly helpful curator of archives and manuscripts at Pitts Theology Library, Robert Presutti, went to extraordinary lengths to make materials available, even going so far as to cart boxes of annual reports to my office to save me the few yards' walk from the Administration Building to Pitts.

The staff of the Manuscript, Archives, and Rare Book Library (MARBL) at Emory have demonstrated once again their invaluable gifts of professionalism, patience, and plain-old helpfulness: John Bence, Erika Bruchko, Elizabeth Chase (now at Stonehill College), Agnieszka Czeblakow, Kate Donovan (now at New York University), Gabrielle Dudley, David Faulds, Catherine Fernandez (now at Princeton), Sarah Logue, and Kathleen Shoemaker.

I am grateful to President Jim Wagner of Emory for his encouragement of this project and for his patience as I have diverted time to it that might otherwise have served the Office of the President.

Finally, since Boone M. Bowen dedicated his history of Candler "to the more than four thousand graduates . . . who have preached and practiced The Gospel," I echo him by dedicating this book to them and to the thousands more who have graduated since 1974. I dedicate this work, moreover, to my wife, Sara Haigh Hauk, to whom I owe more than I can express.

# It may be the defining irony of the Candler School of Theology that

- A conserving impulse led to the founding of a transforming institution.
- The urgency of ministering to Southern Methodism ended up helping it to embrace change.
- The imperative of perpetuating a training school for preachers fostered an institution that would join the foremost ranks of scholarship in theology and religion.

The founders might be surprised, but perhaps not entirely, for they were Christians, adherents to a faith that proclaimed something new in the world and, thus, planted seeds of change in human hearts and society. What might surprise those founders, though, is the degree to which both sides of the irony have lived together successfully through the decades, as conserving and transforming provide each other balance, ministry and prophecy walk hand in hand, and preaching and scholarship inform one another. The school created a hundred years ago has provided a home for reflection, critical study, and inspiration to men and women from many walks of faith, including every expression of Methodism.

The Candler School of Theology had its genesis in the reaction of Southern Methodist bishops against reform-minded educational leaders at Vanderbilt University. When the Methodist Episcopal Church, South, established Candler as the first school of a new university to be called Emory, the church intended to perpetuate what it feared it had lost—a first-rate school for training ministers how to preach and how to care for the Methodist people of the South. The church acted out of nostalgia as much as vision. While the aim was to build a school and a university that would stand for truth and righteousness in education, truth and righteousness already were well defined in the minds of the founders.

As one of them—Asa Griggs Candler—put it in a letter offering a million dollars for the new educational endeavor,

> I desire that whatever I am able to invest in the work of education shall be administered by the Church with a definite and continuous religious purpose. . . . I cannot believe that the promotion of the evangelical and brotherly type of Christianity for which [Methodism] stands will fail to benefit the people of my section and country without regard to denominational lines. This type of Christianity has prevailed generally in the South, and I desire to do what I may be able, to perpetuate it, believing as I do, that it makes for a wholesome conservatism politically and socially, and for a blessed civilization crowned with piety and peace.

From the beginning, however, tension existed between this yearning to hold fast to a threatened way of life and the recognition that holding on would require new ways of thinking about that life, new methods of understanding its source, and new language to speak about hitherto unknown phenomena. The faculty of the school understood this tension as well as anyone, and for that reason they have been, from the beginning, vigorous participants in a long cultural debate, not only in the Southeast but in

America and the church generally. Indeed, the Candler faculty has often modeled this debate within itself, as different theological perspectives emerged to push intellect, in service to faith, toward new kinds of ministry.

This debate—really a deeply searching and respectful conversation throughout the life of Candler—manifested itself in the efforts of the first faculty members to defend themselves, somewhat disingenuously, against charges of modernism. Later on, the faculty acknowledged a growing importance of understanding the people to whom Candler graduates were being sent as ministers; this acknowledgment led the faculty to create a curriculum replete with such disciplines as sociology, psychology, and anthropology—disciplines superficially remote from the gospel but useful to carrying it into new realms. Later still, the effort to live faithfully by Christian principles—indeed, by the rule of the Methodist *Book of Discipline*—prompted the faculty and many students to agitate against the strictures of racial segregation. Still later, a theology of liberation and a theology of hope propelled the school toward greater freedom for women as students and faculty members. Along the way, greater attention to modern media, to the arts, and to the possibilities of collaboration with law, business, public health, nursing, and medicine prompted experiments in programming and outreach that left a stamp on the school and fostered a culture of religious study at Emory perhaps unique in American higher education.

Yet the journey from 1914 to 2014 can hardly be said to have followed an unimpeded erosion of the founders' conserving principle. Throughout its first century, the Candler School of Theology has made room for—indeed has welcomed—a variety of voices and thought. In the same decade when a relatively liberal scholar like Andrew Sledd, the first professor of New Testament at Candler, could proclaim Christianity's "dynamic process of becoming" against the South's "fossil form of doctrine," the presiding influence over the school was that of Sledd's father-in-law, Bishop Warren Candler, a starchy advocate of Wesleyan orthodoxy. At the same time that some members of the Candler faculty were speaking out in defense of the radical theology of the early 1960s, the dean of Candler was a conservative churchman who defended academic freedom as well as the traditions of the church. And just as the demographics of the church—"neither Jew nor gentile, neither slave nor free, neither male nor female"—came to be further defined in terms of denominational affiliation, race, and sexual orientation, that redefinition encountered questions and rejoinder, in the church broadly and in the school itself.

Theologically as well as socially and politically, the tensions within Candler have enlivened the school's teaching and scholarship. But perhaps the most significant thing about these tensions is that they have rarely threatened the collegiality of the faculty or severely eroded the ethos of the Candler community. As one distinguished German theologian put it after visiting Candler in the 1960s, nowhere else in America or Europe had he encountered a faculty so deeply engaged in discussion among themselves about matters of theological substance. A century of conversation and theological exploration has enriched the ongoing contributions of Candler to the life of the church in America and to the intellectual vibrancy of Emory University. This book aims to tell the story of that cultivation of a distinctive mission and ethos.

*Bishop Warren Akin Candler 1875C, president of Emory College from 1888 to 1898 and a leading conservative bishop of the Methodist Episcopal Church, South, led the charge against Vanderbilt University.*

## CHAPTER ONE

# In the Beginning

THE story begins with a kind of game of musical chairs. There were three empty seats and six men willing to occupy them, but a dispute arose about which three men rightly belonged in them. The time was 1910 at Vanderbilt University.

The dispute has been exhaustively recounted in Paul K. Conklin's thorough history, *Gone with the Ivy: A Biography of Vanderbilt University*, as well as in histories of Emory University. For the reader unfamiliar with the tale, the almost impossibly complex story can be summarized succinctly.

The roots of Vanderbilt University reach back before the Civil War, when leaders of the Methodist Episcopal Church, South (MECS), first proposed building a flagship institution of higher education for the church. The war disrupted this initiative, but plans had resumed by 1872 and taken the shape of a charter for Central University, so named because of its location in Nashville, the geographical and publishing center of the MECS. A short year later, the trustees of the university changed its name to recognize the gift of an actual campus and an endowment from the shipping and railroad magnate Cornelius Vanderbilt, "The Commodore." Over the next four years, by the time of his death in 1877, the Commodore gave nearly a million dollars to the university, out of an impulse to reconcile North and South and to honor his second wife (a southern belle, from Mobile, Alabama).

By 1900 the success of the university and its growing reputation had led its young second chancellor, James H. Kirkland, to reach toward greater academic renown, especially in fields where the church had less to sow and less to reap. He would achieve success in reaching this goal with the help of another northern

philanthropist, the agnostic industrialist Andrew Carnegie. This move—together with a growing sense on the part of the church that its child was growing up and perhaps preparing to leave home—spurred the bishops of the MECS to take a tighter hold on the reins they thought they gripped. To their consternation, these reins turned out to be flimsier than they had realized and were held, in fact, by other hands.

The Vanderbilt board of trust, as it is called, sought to remove the reins from the church. When, in 1910, the bishops elected three men to fill vacancies on the board, the board refused to seat them; instead, it elected its own three candidates for those empty places. In the ensuing struggle for supremacy in guiding the future of the university, the Vanderbilt board and the MECS took their argument to chancery court and eventually to the Supreme Court of the state of Tennessee. In March 1914 a majority decision of the court, written by Justice William R. Turner, recognized Cornelius Vanderbilt as the true founder of the university (the church, after all, had

*Asa Griggs Candler, founder of The Coca-Cola Company and older brother of Warren Candler, chaired the Emory board of trustees from 1906 until his death in 1929.*

given less than twenty-five thousand dollars to the university by 1900—about what it later paid in legal costs for its lawsuit) and upheld the claims of the Vanderbilt board to the right to appoint its own members without church approval. The decision dealt a demoralizing blow to the church, and in bitter anger the bishops of the church set about severing for good the MECS relationship with the university.

To compound misfortune, a further problem presented itself to the church. Without Vanderbilt, uncertainty arose about what would become of the theological training of Southern Methodist ministers. Since its founding, Vanderbilt had done a new thing for Southern Methodism: the university had served as the principal site of formal education for ministers filling Southern Methodist pulpits. At the MECS General Conference of 1866, held in New Orleans, the bishops had recommended establishing a seminary devoted exclusively to the education of clergy. As a compromise—because they feared the damping effect of seminary training on the spirited fervor of good preaching, as well as what they supposed to be the dangers of liberalizing scholarship and thinking in seminaries—the majority of the delegates rejected the notion of forming a seminary. Instead, they urged the many small MECS colleges, scattered throughout the South, to take on the role of educating clergy by appointing professors of biblical studies. Over the next forty-eight years, no college did so thorough a job of formally preparing ministers as Vanderbilt. Its Biblical Department developed not only residential programs that enrolled dozens of students but also a correspondence school that became an approved pathway to ordination and that enrolled, astonishingly, more than a thousand students within its first five years.

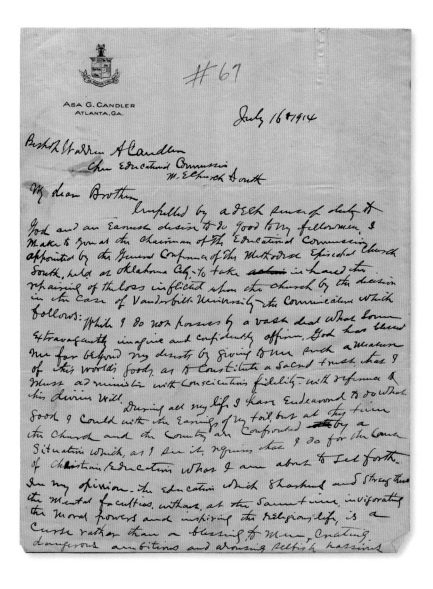

Clearly, the 1914 split with Vanderbilt meant that the church would need to replace the loss of this important school for imbuing ministers with sufficient knowledge and professional skill to care for the souls of the rising middle class in the South. The General Conference of the MECS appointed an Educational Commission and gave it an immediate task: to ensure that theological education would continue by establishing two new theology schools in two new universities, one in the Southwest and one in the Southeast. (Southern Methodist University conveniently had been in development for several years and became the logical candidate to fill that southwestern role.)

Some would say it was a lucky thing, some would say it was providential, that the chair of the Educational Commission was an Emory College alumnus, one of the leading lights in the Southern church, and a younger brother of one of the wealthiest Methodists in the South, if not the entire country. Bishop Warren Akin Candler had graduated from Emory in 1875, at the tender age of eighteen, and

*As the Educational Commission of the Methodist Episcopal Church, South, weighed the advantages of Birmingham, Alabama, against those of Atlanta for the location of the church's new school of theology, Coca-Cola founder Asa Candler helped seal the decision with his "Million Dollar Letter"—postmarked Atlanta.*

*Wyatt Aiken Smart, one of the first seven faculty members at Candler, continued teaching after being appointed university chaplain in 1945, the first person to serve in that position.*

had returned to Oxford, Georgia, a mere thirteen years later to assume the presidency of his alma mater. The school at the time was still struggling to reconstruct itself after the Civil War had left it bankrupt. Candler held the job for a decade, during which he substantially bolstered the college's academic reputation, repaired its creaky financial foundation, and generally prepared it well to step into the twentieth century. Perhaps as a foreshadowing, among the academic improvements Candler brought to Emory during his presidency was the creation of a theology department.

Candler's election as bishop in 1898 was greeted by rousing cheers from the students. Although they were sorry to lose "King Shorty," as they affectionately called the five-and-a-half-foot-tall Candler, they believed that the church had ratified the quality of their president and, thus, the excellence of their college and of them.

Although several cities quickly presented themselves in 1914 as suitable sites for the new southeastern university, the Educational Commission, chaired by Candler, just as quickly eliminated most of them, and soon the contest came down to Birmingham, Alabama—where Southern College, now Birmingham-Southern University, offered an inviting campus—and Atlanta. (In that same year, coincidentally, the Presbyterians also were campus shopping and planning to move Oglethorpe University from Milledgeville to Atlanta.)

What led the Educational Commission to choose Atlanta over Birmingham was an alluring letter from Bishop Candler's older brother Asa, founder of The Coca-Cola Company, who offered a million dollars in cash to launch the university. The Atlanta Chamber of Commerce also pledged half a million dollars to help locate the university in Atlanta, and other advantages like transportation and financial services favored the Phoenix City, so-called for its rise from the ashes of the Civil War. Asa Candler would later sweeten his own offer with seventy-five acres of land in suburban Atlanta. It could not have been an accident that his initial gift was a bit more than what Commodore Vanderbilt had given to Central University some forty years earlier.

While the 1914 victory of Vanderbilt University over the church ignited anger among Southern Methodists, it also fired up their determination to forge new means for building what Henry Luce would later term "the American century." These Methodists might also dare hope that it would also be the "Methodist century." The previous half-century, since the end of the Civil War, had brought the ascension of Methodism as the most populous denomination in the country and, in many ways, the most influential and most representative. Thoroughly middle-class, Methodism gave to its people a high regard for the transformative power of education, in behalf of individual souls and the reformation of society. The denomination inherited this faith from John Wesley, the founding genius of Methodism. In turn, Methodism both north and south absorbed the national ethos of democratic pragmatism. Nothing accommodated that ethos quite so well as the many regional conferences that constituted the governing structure of Methodism.

The time was thus ripe, in 1914, for the Methodist Episcopal Church, South, to plant educational institutions in two American cities that appeared to epitomize pragmatic American striving at the turn of the twentieth century: Dallas and Atlanta. By 1914 both cities had developed into regional anchors for transportation, finance, manufacturing, and trade. Each was the largest city in its state, and each was home to the headquarters of an episcopal area for the Southern Methodist Church— for Dallas, the North Texas Conference, and for Atlanta, the North Georgia Conference.

By a happy convergence of circumstances, the same reforming forces that helped to wrest Vanderbilt University from the grasp of the church may have prepared the way for the founding of Southern Methodist University and Emory University. One such force was the push for standardized educational expectations in the professions, a development that led to new institutional arrangements to meet those expectations. At Vanderbilt, Andrew Carnegie's insistence that the medical school be unencumbered by a sectarian governing board was part of what precipitated the split with the church. Similarly, a report on American medical education prepared in 1910 by Abraham Flexner for the Carnegie Foundation (there was that name again) recommended, among other improvements, that all proprietary medical schools in the country should become affiliated with universities to shore up the education of doctors in the basic sciences. In Atlanta this recommendation led to the merger of the Atlanta Medical College (founded in 1854) with the newly chartered Emory University in 1915.

## Junior Class

*Plato Durham offered a cartoonist's view of seminary juniors for the Emory University yearbook,* The Campus.

In the ministry as well, rising expectations among middle-class congregations required that their pastors should have not only the social cachet that came with college education but also a deeper understanding of the emerging disciplines of psychology, sociology, and historical criticism. This impetus had led to the designation of Vanderbilt itself as the central university in Southern Methodism for educating

## Middle Class

*Perhaps in Durham's view the second-year students at Candler disregarded their studies for other priorities.*

clergy. When the MECS lost control over that institution, the church felt an immediate imperative to fill the void, so as to continue meeting the pastoral needs of its people. The historian Glenn T. Miller has noted that the newly emergent American university—which brought together the undergraduate college with graduate and professional schools—admirably suited the aims of a denomination like Methodism, whose roots were "deeply reformist and deeply committed to America's possibilities." The undergraduate college would lift people up; the professional schools would prepare them to change the world.

As the new theology school in Atlanta would demonstrate, however, the "deeply reformist" instincts of Methodism held the seeds of theological, political, and social tension and even conflict. Such a reformist cause as the temperance movement, for instance, had both conservative and progressive tendencies. On the one hand, the movement derived much of its initiative, energy, and creative genius from women, although episcopal leaders like Warren Candler certainly spoke in behalf of the aims of the movement. On the other hand, someone as conservative as Candler could hardly tolerate the degree to which the movement progressively brought women into the political sphere, which in his view belonged to men. This tension between conservatism and progressivism would play out significantly—in rather healthy and constructive ways—in the theology faculty in coming decades. But in the meantime, a new school needed to be launched.

Following the ruling of the Tennessee Supreme Court in favor of Vanderbilt on March 21, 1914, events developed quickly. Within weeks the General Conference of the church agreed in a close vote (153-132) to sever all ties with Vanderbilt, and the conference subsequently charged the Educational Commission. Meeting in Birmingham, Alabama, on June 17, the commission agreed that its first step should be to establish a theology school in the Southeast.

A month later, on July 16, 1914, meeting in Atlanta, the commission received the so-called million-dollar letter from Asa Candler, a member of the commission. The decision settled, there was little time to spare in laying the groundwork for the new university. The Educational Commission appointed Bishop Warren Candler to serve as the university's chancellor (borrowing the Vanderbilt University term for its chief executive) and to hire a theology faculty to begin instruction in September.

In naming Bishop Candler to his post, the commission chose astutely on two counts. For one thing, as a former president of Emory College who had put it on sound financial footing, raised its academic standards, and enhanced the prospects of private higher education throughout Georgia in various ways, he came to the role of chancellor with certifiable administrative and educational bona fides. At the same time, his close relationship with his wealthy brother Asa, and the high regard for Warren throughout the church and in Atlanta, meant that he would bring many allies to the purpose of ensuring Emory University's success.

The first biography of Warren Candler, published in 1948, seven years after his death, was titled *Giant Against the Sky,* a phrase that suggests the high esteem in which the Southern Methodist Church held him as an episcopal leader in a period of great moment for the nation and the church—and, hence, the singular appropriateness of applying his name to the new school of theology.

Hardly systematic or original in his theology, he taught and preached Wesleyan doctrinal purity. For him the Bible unveiled an orthodox truth about "the faith once given." Although antimodernist and "antiliberalist" (in his term), he nevertheless was hospitable to any nuggets of truth that could be found in liberalism—for he recognized that the gospel itself planted seeds of change. Skeptical of human capacity for goodness apart from the ancient Christian faith (especially as carried forward by Methodism), he opposed what he called the "soap and soup religion" of the Social Gospel. To him, social redemption began with personal redemption; human welfare would derive from the triumph of the kingdom of God, which depends not on social action or the hard work of the church but on individual regeneration and the saving grace of God. If modern society were to avoid the burdens of the capitalist/industrialist age, it would do so by means of a "return to Wesley's God," whose mercy makes "the divine fatherhood and human brotherhood" real. This was Warren Candler's central message in the Episcopal Address he delivered to the MECS General Conference in 1914—an address that the church printed in half a million copies.

## Senior Class

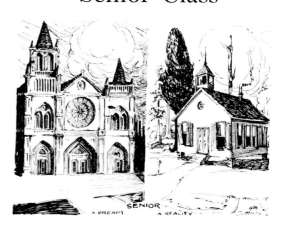

*Durham well understood the path that most Candler students would follow after graduation.*

Charged as chancellor to appoint a faculty, Bishop Candler lacked the requisite academic credentials but possessed a keen sense of what the church needed. He was not himself a scholar in any serious sense. He was a prolific preacher, author, pamphleteer, and lecturer, who marshaled great natural intelligence and energy in behalf of "the faith once for all delivered to the saints." So it is fair to say that in choosing a faculty he had less of an academic aim in mind than an ecclesiastical one. Nevertheless, Bishop Candler's early appointments helped establish some of the directions and themes for which the Candler School of Theology would become well known, especially its reputation for formative teaching and its emphasis on scholarship that was both groundbreaking and church-renewing. All of the first seven faculty members were devoted to Methodism as it found its expression in the MECS, but they did not always conform in their teaching or in their extracurricular work to the ideals of Bishop Candler.

The first dean of the school, Plato Tracy Durham, was integral to its formation from the start. He served as secretary of the Educational Commission and thus became one of the first trustees of the new university before he was asked to step into the role of dean of theology. Hailing from North Carolina, Durham lacked a doctoral degree but had graduated from Trinity College (now Duke University) and studied at Yale Divinity School and Oxford University. His courses in church history made him one of the most sought-after teachers on the faculty. This popularity may have been because, as his colleague Professor William Shelton later said of him, the past was still alive for Durham: "the dead were only for a time just out of sight." He infused his lectures with a sense of the numinous. Shelton noted, wryly, that Durham was constantly "talking about the cosmic: the cosmic soul, the cosmic God, the cosmic Christ, and few knew what he meant but everyone who knew him well knew that he meant something."

Among the groundbreaking activities of Durham's career—including an old-fashioned campus revival in 1920 that was remembered for decades—none may have been as significant as his serving as cofounder of the Commission on Interracial Cooperation in 1919. A son of the South who loved his native region, he nevertheless planted seeds of social reform

*Plato Tracy Durham served as the first dean of the Candler School of Theology.*

and racial justice, including the beginnings of collaboration with historically black colleges in Atlanta. In his last public appearance, he offered the keynote address at a ceremony honoring Dr. John Hope, president of Morehouse College, in which he applauded the work of Hope in behalf of African Americans as a way of emancipating whites. Durham died the next day, February 10, 1930, at age fifty-seven.

William Arthur Shelton, appointed to the professorship of Hebrew and Old Testament Literature, had earned his BD and MA at Yale before serving pastorates in the Indian Territory (later Oklahoma) for twelve years. His passion for the pastorate was equaled, however, by his passion for ancient languages and civilizations. In 1920 he was the sole scholar not from the University of Chicago invited to join the American Scientific Expedition to the Middle East, the first such excursion to a land recently freed by

*Andrew Sledd, son-in-law of Bishop Candler, had been fired by the Emory College board in 1902 in response to public outrage over his antilynching article in the Atlantic. He was among the first theology faculty members hired by Candler in 1914.*

World War I from the rule of the Ottoman Empire. While in Egypt, Iraq, Palestine, and Lebanon, Shelton collected and sent home to Atlanta antiquities that became the nucleus of the Emory Museum, now the Michael C. Carlos Museum. His account of the expedition, in his book *Dust and Ashes of Empires*, brings a highly literate and richly historical sensitivity to the sort of awe that would become part of later-twentieth-century Holy Land tours. Yet it is clear from his account of the exodus in this book that his understanding of biblical history took a critical approach quite at odds with literalist interpretations. He understood biblical history to be the unfolding story of the human encounter with the divine and a deepening, evolving understanding of that encounter. In this thinking he was more in tune with the liberal theology then ascendant in America than with the Protestant orthodoxy of the previous century (or of his chancellor).

Andrew Sledd, the first person chosen for the faculty of the new school, was the only member of the original Candler faculty to have earned a PhD. He also happened to be the son-in-law of Chancellor Candler, though scholarly capability no doubt trumped nepotism in the appointment. Sledd's story has been well chronicled in Emory histories. He was teaching Latin at Emory College in 1902 when he published an article in the *Atlantic Monthly* that challenged his native South to abide by the rule of law and denounce the practice of lynching African Americans. The article created a sense of regional betrayal and outrage among the Georgia populace, a fury exacerbated by the racist demagoguery of several powerful and longtime antagonists of

*The Wesley Memorial Building, whose auditorium is shown here, served as the first home of the Candler School of Theology, from 1914 to 1916.*

Bishop Candler. To avoid what it thought would be an embarrassment to the college, the Emory board of trustees demanded Sledd's resignation. He went on from that humiliation to earn his PhD from Yale and to serve as president of the University of Florida and later of Southern University in Alabama.

The formation of the new theology school in Atlanta provided Sledd's father-in-law—Bishop Candler—an opportunity to offer redemption to Emory. Sledd not only raised the school's reputation for scholarship (he was one of only fifteen scholars from North America invited to prepare the new American Revised Standard Version of the Bible in the 1930s) but also left a profound legacy of advocacy for racial justice. His impact on race relations can be measured in part by the white ministers who attended the memorial service for four black girls killed in a church bombing in Birmingham in 1963. As recounted by Bishop Kenneth Goodson, those ministers were "almost to a man students of Andrew Sledd."

Although Shelton had established an academic reputation as an archaeologist and interpreter of Hebrew scripture, and Sledd was widely recognized as a New Testament scholar, the rest of the faculty, while broadly educated, could not have been called specialized scholars in any modern sense. As one of them, Wyatt Aiken Smart, would write forty-three years later, "At least half of them had never taught at all, and the rest had taught only college courses in religion for comparatively short periods. . . . In the main, they were successful preachers, chosen to teach young men how to become successful preachers."

But Sledd can stand as a kind of paradigm of the faculty in Candler's first century. He was sometimes at odds with his fellow faculty members, as the next chapter shows. His commitment to the church did not undermine his theological sophistication or the soundness of his scholarship—quite the opposite. It spurred his dedication to trying to get theology and scholarship right. According to Thomas Trotter, Sledd's impact on biblical scholarship in the 1937–75 period can be seen in the careers of some of the students he taught, including Albert Edward Barnett 21T, Ernest

Cadman Colwell 23T 27T 44H, John Knox 24T 56H, and Albert C. Outler 33T. Recalling Sledd's influence, Outler later categorized Sledd as a kind of "academic missionary" whose aim was to free his native region, the South, from "literalism and traditionalism." This missionary zeal among some Candler faculty would cause consternation in the decades to come, but in August 1914 those problems were still far off.

The rest of the first faculty included Hugh Henry Harris, a professor of sociology (unusual for the time; Harris also was the only Yankee on the first faculty); Wyatt Aiken Smart, a professor of biblical theology, who would deliver the 1940 Lyman Beecher Lectures and later serve as Emory University's first chaplain (1945-52); Henry Clay Howard, a professor of systematic theology who would become the first pastor of Emory Methodist Church, now Glenn Memorial; and William James Young, a professor of homiletics and pastoral theology, whose own account of his life took greatest pride in the churches he had served in Texas, Virginia, and Maryland.

Bishop Candler demonstrated a remarkable intuition about the capacity of the faculty members he chose. Astonishingly, these newly minted professors—with little experience of what a seminary curriculum should look like beyond their own schooling—hammered together a respectable course of study in just a month. Taking their cues from seminaries elsewhere, the faculty organized themselves into disciplinary areas: biblical studies, systematic theology, church history, homiletics, and sociology/religious education. The curricula for both the diploma and the bachelor of divinity degree offered tracks leading to four possible vocations: pastor, missionary, social service, and religious education. From the beginning, then, the school recognized that most of its students would be headed to local churches or the mission field, but it also intended to train teachers and leaders of organizations like the YMCA and the YWCA. The school also offered the MA in each of these tracks, even before Emory University organized its graduate school in 1919.

With mere weeks to prepare for the first year of instruction in the school, Bishop Candler turned to a facility that he knew well—Wesley Memorial Church. Founded in downtown Atlanta in 1902 as a halfway point between Trinity Methodist, near the Georgia capitol, and First Methodist, at the corner of Peachtree Street and what is now Ralph McGill Boulevard, the church had dedicated a new building at the corner of Auburn Avenue and Ivy Street (now Peachtree Center Avenue) in 1910. Bishop Candler had overseen design and construction of Wesley Memorial, whose large auditorium and many offices not only offered sanctuary to the North Georgia Conference until the 1960s but also conveniently accommodated the sixty-nine

Henry Hornbostel's original campus plan for the Atlanta campus of Emory University shows the theology building in the lower left corner. Much of the plan remained unbuilt, but the campus conforms rather well a century later to Hornbostel's ideal.

students who enrolled for the first quarter of the new theology school in 1914.

Those students arrived in Atlanta with varying levels of preparation. Some had been students at Vanderbilt and decided to continue their studies at the new school. Many had no college degrees and therefore followed the diploma track, which required no bachelor's degree and excused the students from learning Hebrew and Greek. The rest—a few—brought with them collegiate preparation and aimed for the bachelor of divinity degree. Altogether three would graduate the following year during the commencement activities at Oxford, where Emory College remained until 1919. Those first three graduates included one receiving the diploma (Arthur P. Ratledge) and two receiving the BD, Robert H. Ruff and Keener L. Rudolph. Both Ruff and Rudolph would later become college presidents. By virtue of the alphabet, Rudolph became the first divinity graduate of Candler, and by virtue of paternity he helped to contribute to the current architectural look of Emory by fathering Paul Rudolph, the architect who designed Cannon Chapel in the 1970s.

The new university did not operate under a charter until the following January, with the name of Emory carried over from the college, and in February 1915 the university trustees (all members of the Educational Commission) agreed to name the new theology school Candler—presumably to honor the bishop, though the minutes do not specify whether it was Warren or Asa or both whose name would be enshrined.

Because the Educational Commission had designated fully half of Asa Candler's million-dollar gift to the theology school for endowment, the school began on a solid foundation. Tuition cost nothing for those first students, and while the first bulletin of the school projected fees, books, room, and board to cost a modest $187 for three quarters, the trustees still set aside scholarships of up to $100 to offset the burden for less-than-affluent budding ministers.

In a more concrete vein—really a vein of marble, quarried in North Georgia—construction of the school's new campus in Druid Hills was under way. The first two academic buildings were dedicated to use by the Candler School of Theology and the Lamar School of Law (named at that time for L. Q. C. Lamar 1845C and a U.S. Supreme Court justice until his death in 1893; this usage was later dropped). Mirror images, the schools of theology and law faced one another across the Quadrangle. Designed by Henry Hornbostel, the buildings included subtle touches that signified their respective areas of study. Up under the eaves of the law school building—now Carlos Hall—the soffit is punctuated by molded concrete icons alternating between an image of the tablets of the Mosaic law and an image of the scales of justice. On the Theology Building, the icons along the soffit alternate between a Celtic cross (the Candler family hailed four generations back from Scotland) and the crown of thorns. By the time the school moved into its new quarters on the Druid Hills campus in 1916, two dormitories also had been completed to house theology students—Dobbs Hall and Winship Hall (Winship was demolished in 1984 to make way for the Dobbs University Center). The Theology Building housed not only classrooms and faculty offices but also the theology library (only several thousand books at the time), the imposing office of Chancellor Warren Candler, and a chapel whose interior was clad in marble. The chapel was later named for Dean Durham.

The school occupied its building in September 1916, in time for its third academic year. Enrollment that year grew to 134, of whom 59 had graduated from college and 58 others had some college education. Unfortunately, the following April ushered the United States into World War I, and enrollment in every school of the university dropped for the duration of the war—most dramatically in the law and medical schools, but in the theology school as well, as the number of Candler students fell to 111. A year later, in the fall of 1918, enrollment fell to 77, as ordained clergy entered military chaplaincy, while prospective theology students replaced them in local pulpits.

The fall of 1918 also brought the resignation of Dean Durham, whose gifts apparently lay in teaching and preaching, not in administration. Confronted with what amounted to a mutiny in the November faculty meeting, the dean learned that if he did not resign, his entire faculty would do so because of his administrative performance. (No minutes of the meeting exist, so the specific source of the faculty's unhappiness is unclear.) Hugh Henry Harris, professor of religious education and sociology, stepped in until the end of the term, and beginning in 1919 Franklin Nutting Parker succeeded to the deanship by appointment of the chancellor.

Thus, in five short years the Candler School of Theology not only had hired its first faculty and enrolled its first students, but also had moved from one campus to another and weathered its first faculty revolt. The school was maturing quickly. *C*

*Franklin Nutting Parker served as the second dean of the
theology school but declined election as bishop.*

## CHAPTER TWO

# MODERN TWENTIES, DEPRESSED THIRTIES

WITH the theology school fully in operation after five years of great expenditure of energy, the faculty and administration of Candler had little opportunity to mark time and watch the 1920s unfold. They had cultural upheaval to address.

Along with the slaughtering of millions of young men, World War I brought the death of a great many ideals and hopes. In some minds November 1918 and the armistice also brought the end of the nineteenth century—a century that included more than its share of imperialism and Western hubris as well as an abundance of social optimism, Protestant ascendancy, progressive ideals, and theological liberalism. By 1920 the wave of hope on which the churches, the Social Gospel, and the progressive movement had ridden through the late nineteenth and early twentieth centuries was crashing against the realities of vast social and intellectual dislocations. The publication of *The Waste Land* by T. S. Eliot in 1922 spoke for many on both sides of the Atlantic in its evocation of a world whose foundation had been wrecked.

As the churches in America made the transition from the progressive era to this new and anxious decade, their stock in some parts of society fell. They were viewed by many as purveyors of folly, of either pie in the sky or vain, human dreams of utopia. Spurred by social critics like H. L. Mencken and Walter Lippmann, American intellectuals began to view religion with a gimlet eye. In fact, disappointment in the church may have helped the sales of one of the most

popular novels of the decade–Sinclair Lewis's *Elmer Gantry*, in which a womanizing Methodist preacher hustles a good living by less than ethical means.

One response to world changes took the form of Karl Barth's *Epistle to the Romans*, which ushered in a period of theological neoorthodoxy. Barth's theology amounted to a rejection of natural theology, or the notion that God was immanent in the world and could be found, understood, and defended through human reason. Barth also called into question every human enterprise, over against which God stood as the unfathomable Other, in transcendent judgment and revelation–judgment of human pride, revelation of human need for divine grace. In Barth's view the liberal theology of the previous decades had overestimated the human capacity to accomplish God's purposes on earth. Liberal theology had even assumed–wrongly, according to Barth– that humans could know God's purposes. Barth believed that divine purpose is

*By 1922 the campus of Emory University in the Druid Hills section of Atlanta had lost little of its expansive woodlands. The Theology Building is shown at left.*

revealed not in nature but in a radical divine word that contradicts human aspiration and human folly (which are the same).

Another, quite different response to the modern world that presented itself at the close of World War I came in the guise of a renewed and invigorated fundamentalism. Among the fantastic coincidences attending the birth of the Candler School of Theology, none cut as close to the bone as the publication of *The Fundamentals*, a twelve-volume series of essays whose last volume appeared in July 1915. The term "fundamentalist" itself was coined as the new decade began in 1920.

Fueled largely by northern and midwestern churches in reaction to the growth of liberal theology in their denominations in the previous two decades, and responding also to a growing secularism in those regions of the country, fundamentalism had taken root more slowly in the South. There, the churches had resisted liberalism and had persisted longer in the old Calvinist dispensation that saw the Bible as a purveyor of consistent doctrine from Genesis to Revelation. "Old-time" religion had long helped to buttress a conservative hold on other dimensions of culture and had thereby resisted some of the calls of liberal theology for social action. Having experienced the destruction of one way of life in the Civil War, the South needed little prodding to oppose the encroachments of modern "isms," including Darwinism, biblical criticism, Bolshevism, "Romanism" (Catholicism), and other trends that had more to do with American culture than with church doctrine. Yet as fundamentalism gained a foothold in the South, it wagged its finger at two institutions in particular—liberal churches, where doctrine seemed to be indifferently defended, and schools of theology, where doctrine seemed to be threatened by new forms of study and knowledge.

At Candler in the 1920s, the prevailing theological view among the faculty ranged well within the margins of these two very different critiques of modernity— the Barthian on one hand and the fundamentalist on the other. The irony is that the school suffered different kinds of opprobrium for its attempt at forging a middle ground. From the fundamentalist side the school was feared as a wellspring of liberal theology, and from the side of the new orthodoxy it was looked down upon as—well, the last bastion of liberal theology.

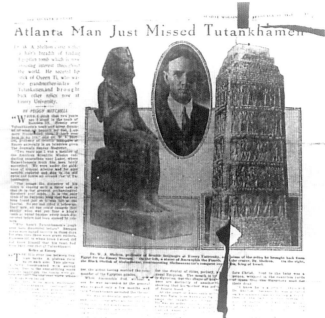

*This* Atlanta *newspaper article by the later author of* Gone with the Wind *tells the story of a Candler faculty member's close brush with* King Tut.

*Durham Chapel, named for the first dean of Candler, provided sanctuary for worship for sixty years before renovations to the Theology Building filled this space with shelves and books to expand Pitts Theology Library.*

The situation might be exemplified by Candler's new dean (as of January 1919), Franklin Nutting Parker, who was also the professor of systematic theology. Parker would have found himself at home teaching theology in nineteenth-century Emory College, and those nineteenth-century students would likely have found him appealing. In his 1924 book *What We Believe: Studies in Christian Doctrine*, he elaborates upon the articles of the Apostles' Creed. Tellingly, the book is dedicated to the conservative bishop Warren Akin Candler, "great preacher and able defender of the faith once given in Jesus Christ Our Lord." Drawing heavily on the Wesleyan tradition that "faith and knowledge work together," Parker emphasizes both the need and the possibility of "making harmony between mind and heart." The book is thus very much in Wesley's tradition of equipping the faithful and is, in fact, a kind of catechetical resource.

In the book Parker holds very closely to an evangelical brand of liberal theology. His faith in reason is such that he espouses the "evidences of Christianity" in nature and conscience that had been around for the previous century and had formed a part of the college curriculum. Yet he also emphasizes the atoning work of Jesus and the need for the human soul to experience repentance and regeneration. His faith in the church is such that he is able to speak confidently of Christianity triumphant over other religions this side of God's kingdom, yet he also holds forth the understanding that "each new age needs to consider the doctrine [of the atonement] under the conditions of its own time." His ecclesiology is deeply informed by the Articles of Faith of Methodism and by the Wesleyan "reclaiming" of the prospect of "going on to perfection." Exemplifying the sort of rhetorical gifts expected of a homiletician of the day, he quotes freely from Wordsworth, Tennyson, Browning, and Shakespeare, often concluding his chapters—as he might finish up a sermon—with a reflection on a bit of English verse.

For theologians forging the paths of thought that would predominate in divinity schools later in the century, such a systematic theology would have appeared regressive and, in fact, even unhelpful in a pastoral sense. It would not, indeed could not, speak to doubting minds or to intellectual sensibilities assaulted by what the first decades of the century had wrought.

Yet it was not to those sensibilities that the school principally aimed to minister. It was to other sensibilities, which were offended largely by rumors of the theology faculty's predilection for modernism. And here, ironically, the somewhat old-fashioned systematic theologian and dean found himself in a fight because he was considered to be too liberal. Antimodernism among Methodists in the South stirred

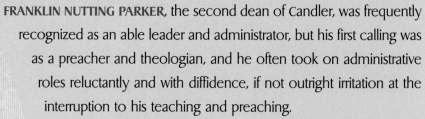

**FRANKLIN NUTTING PARKER,** the second dean of Candler, was frequently recognized as an able leader and administrator, but his first calling was as a preacher and theologian, and he often took on administrative roles reluctantly and with diffidence, if not outright irritation at the interruption to his teaching and preaching.

Born in New Orleans in 1867, Parker attended Centenary College and Tulane University but never earned a degree. (This lack of a credential would not deter the Emory chapter of Phi Beta Kappa from conferring honorary membership on him much later in his life.) After ordination to the Methodist ministry, he served churches in French-speaking parishes of Louisiana, often traveling the bayous by paddlewheel boats. Following appointment to Rayne Memorial in New Orleans, he served for a time as presiding elder of the New Orleans and Baton Rouge districts before accepting appointment as professor of biblical literature at Trinity College (now Duke University) in 1911. Bishop Candler recruited him as professor of systematic theology in 1915, in time to begin the second year of teaching at the school. When Dean Durham resigned in November 1918, Professor Henry Howard was appointed acting dean until January, and then Parker assumed the deanship; he served until 1937. As dean emeritus he continued to teach until retiring in 1942, at age seventy-five.

Once, in 1918, Parker was elected to the episcopacy but declined to serve. According to his own account, he could not answer "yes" to the question asked, during consecration of a bishop, whether he believed that it was "the will of our Lord Jesus Christ" for him to spend the rest of his life as an administrator. Four years later he refused to allow his name even to be put in nomination. Despite being elected to the General Conference seven times, to ecumenical conferences twice, and to the uniting conference of Methodism in 1939, he viewed these assignments not as honors but as jobs to be done for the sake of the church. In 1920, as Bishop Candler insisted on stepping down from the increasingly burdensome role of chancellor of Emory, the trustees turned to Parker, who served as acting chancellor and was urged to take on the new responsibility of president. He declined. Harvey Warren Cox was appointed president of Emory later that year.

In 1940, the clergy of the Southeastern Jurisdiction of the Methodist Church—many of whom had learned theology from Parker—launched a fund-raising campaign to create an endowment for the Franklin N. Parker Chair of Systematic Theology at Candler, the first endowed chair in the theology school. It was a testament to Parker's impact on these former students that they raised one hundred thousand dollars on their clerical salaries to endow the chair fully (about the equivalent of $4 million in 2012 dollars). Mack B. Stokes was the first person appointed to the chair, in 1953.

enough concern in the mind of Dean Parker that he mentioned it several times in his annual reports.

As enrollment dipped in response to the American effort in World War I, Parker noted that the Candler school had difficulty overcoming the decline because clergy and churches were advising prospective ministerial students to look elsewhere. In part this advice had to do with the belief that college graduates could move directly into the pulpit and skip theological education altogether. As Parker reported to the president, "[There is] a very widespread indifference, if not opposition, to specific theological education in our church. In many instances, young men are advised not to go to theological seminaries, but to proceed at once from college into the itinerant ministry."

Another important reason for resistance to sending prospective Methodist ministers to Candler arose from the view that other seminaries would be better at maintaining the spirit, while the mind might take care of itself. Candler was, in the view of many Southern Methodists, simply too "modern." In fact, this perception of modernism in academia had been one of the irritants at Vanderbilt two decades previously—the perception that that university was moving away from traditional values of the rank and file in the church—and it was one of the reasons why the church finally separated from Vanderbilt rather than try to repair the breach from the lost court case. The Candler School of Theology seemed now to be carrying this torch on behalf of Vanderbilt. As Parker noted,

> *There has been for years a continual difficulty growing out of the alleged liberalism of the views and teachings of certain professors in our school. This militates against some students coming here. It has been, [moreover,] a tradition in the Southern Methodist Church that theological seminaries are scarcely needed and a large number of older ministers are utterly opposed to them.*

Which faculty members prompted such fears of modernizing and spirit-damping education?

One was Wyatt Aiken Smart, professor of biblical theology, who embraced literary criticism, historical criticism, and form criticism as ways of trying to understand the meaning of scripture. His stature as a biblical scholar even as early as the first decade of Candler's existence was later confirmed by his invitation to deliver the Cole Lectures at Vanderbilt. The published lectures appeared in 1947 as *Still the Bible Speaks*—not exactly the proclamation of a theological bomb-thrower—and in the

introduction to the book Smart appealed to readers "to let the past speak to the present without enslaving it." His aim was to root the present church firmly in the soil of the past while nurturing the life of the church with the insight offered by more recent discoveries. He aimed to educate a younger generation that appeared to ignore both God and the Word. Along the way, however, he reminded readers that the Bible's word is a religious one, and that Christians should turn to the ancient text for confirmation of their faith, not confirmation of cosmology, geology, or history. His work thus exhibited many of the hallmarks of liberal theology—a recognition that the Bible was not a univocal document, that it was the product of a changing culture, and most of all that it did not contain infallible guidance about the origins or structure of the material world.

Another faculty member viewed as objectionable was Andrew Sledd, who in 1930 published what to twenty-first-century readers would appear to be a wholly uncontroversial history of the Bible titled *The Bibles of the Churches*. In the very first chapter, however, Sledd noted the long and complex centuries of choice in the matter of writings, translations, compilations, and even arrangements of the books of the Bible that make it an ambiguous source of authority. For churchgoers seeking an "inerrant" word, the suggestion of ambiguity became a lightning rod. Sledd also taught the now widely accepted view that the Gospel of John had not been written by the "beloved disciple" but by a late-first-century Hellenistic Jew who had never seen Jesus.

*Looking plenty the worse for wear, the 1933 "Theologs" intramural basketball team appears to have distinguished itself by passive resistance on the court, threatening almost no one.*

In retrospect it may be possible to overstate the theological push of the churches against Candler. Southern Methodism experienced less fundamentalist enthusiasm than churches in the North. Just as critical to the liberal reputation of Candler throughout the South was the social—not theological—liberalism of the school and the university of which it was a part. A kind of civil theology hung over much of the region, which remained largely rural and suspicious of urban developments. While the trustees of Candler and Emory had exercised foresight in establishing these schools in the most booming city in the Southeast, not all of their regional compatriots shared their enthusiasm for the advantages of the city.

The modernist controversy was not merely theological but also social. World War I had incited fierce anti-German sentiment throughout the United States, and for Southern Methodists Germany was not only the seedbed of liberal theology but also the symbol of a beer-drinking culture that needed to be stamped out through Prohibition (such prominent American breweries as Anheuser-Busch had the double damnation of possessing a German name). Other sources of social dislocation lay in the rifts within Southern Methodism itself, as women sought a voice in denominational decisions at the General Conference, and as laity in general sought to curb the authority of the bishops and gain greater representation for themselves.

Not only the theology school but the university as a whole served as targets for brickbats. To shed light on how Emory could serve both Jerusalem and Athens, both the church and the academy, the editors of the *Emory Alumnus* in March 1929 published an editorial distinguishing between a *religious* institution and a *sectarian* one. The bylaws of Emory, they noted, described the university as "a profoundly religious institution without being narrowly sectarian." To that end, said the editorialists, the university's scholars needed "absolute freedom of expression." Again, the bylaws: "[Emory] proposes to encourage freedom of thought as liberal as *the limitations of truth*" (emphasis added). To do that, said the editors, "The University's function is to lead, not to be led."

The theology school harbored a majority of faculty members who took a decidedly progressive view of the freedom to pursue their scholarship unencumbered by the dogma of the previous century. Moreover, the theology faculty allied itself with the progressive side of one of the great issues in Methodism of the day—the reunification of the denomination that had split in 1844 and 1845. Emory in fact lay at the heart of that separation, which had been precipitated by a debate over slavery. In 1844 the president of the Emory College board of trustees, Bishop James O. Andrew of the Methodist Episcopal Church, owned a number of slaves. When his ownership of slaves—in contradiction to long-standing Methodist policy—became an issue at

*(Top)* Candler student Isaac Inouye, a member of the class of 1922 from Hawaii, picked up the mantel from Dean Durham when it came to cartooning for The Campus. *(Middle)* In this cartoon Inouye played on John and Charles Wesley's name for their early Methodist organization at Oxford University, The Holy Club. *(Bottom)* For Inouye—as for others called to Candler—the Cross stood above all the various paths their ministries might take.

the General Conference of the Methodist Episcopal Church, meeting in New York City in 1844, southern delegates refused to support a resolution calling for Bishop Andrew to step down from office or free his slaves. The following year, meeting in Louisville, Kentucky, the southern church organized itself as the Methodist Episcopal Church, South.

As early as 1869 the northern church had proposed reunion, and by 1894 the southern church was ready to begin considering that possibility. By the turn of the century both denominations undertook work in earnest toward developing a plan of unification—a prospect hardly attracting universal endorsement among Southern Methodists. Even the Candler faculty lacked consensus on the matter. Speaking in favor of reunion was William Shelton, professor of Hebrew and Old Testament literature, who traveled in May 1924 to the Methodist Episcopal Church general conference as a "fraternal messenger" appointed by the southern church. His message essentially was, "We are in favor; it's up to you." Indeed this last clause became the title of a pamphlet he published later that year outlining for his fellow southern church members the arguments in favor of reunion.

Some seven months later Shelton's faculty colleague Andrew Sledd produced a rebuttal in the form of an open letter titled "Proof or Propaganda?" In it he scolded Shelton for publishing "misleading implications" and "fancies and fallacies." Sledd viewed as naïve the assumption that northern churches would give up recruiting in the South, and he expressed concern that the united denomination would operate as a racially integrated body. On the issue of race relations Sledd was among the more liberal white southerners of that day, yet even he drew the line at uniting before the question of racial ecclesiology was sorted out.

Bishop Candler also weighed in against reunion. Although he had retired as chancellor of Emory in 1920, he still exerted considerable sway over the theology school, so it could not have escaped notice of faculty and students when he helped form and later chaired the "Association to Preserve and Promote Southern Methodism."

On the other hand, Professor Shelton reported that ten Candler students had signed a statement that racism appeared to be a major factor in the opposition to unification, and that if this sin were indeed the case, they would be seeking ordination in a denomination other than the MEC, South.

In the end, the northern and southern churches moved together during the 1930s, a rapprochement culminating in the joining together of the Methodist Episcopal Church, the MECS, and the Methodist Protestant Church. The unification was

*The chancel of Durham Chapel was clad in marble.*

made possible by a variety of factors, including the waning authority of conservative bishops like Candler, a growing awareness of greater possibility for fulfilling the churches' mission to the world through the sharing of resources, and a brokered agreement that would allow segregation to persist in the southern churches for at least another couple of decades.

If all of this fraught negotiation and parsing of fine points sounds rather Methodist-centric, there is good reason. The Candler School of Theology was not yet the ecumenical haven it would become. Non-Methodist students were not admitted until 1935, and no non-Methodist faculty member was appointed until 1946, in the school's fourth decade.

While the theological and organizational debates about the church engaged the faculty and leadership at Candler during the 1930s, far more urgent local concerns gripped the school and the university. In 1926, moving into the second decade of Emory as a university, the university trustees launched what was then the largest capital campaign ever undertaken in the South, with the aim of raising $10 million in ten years. By the following year the university had raised eight hundred thousand dollars, but very soon there is no further mention of the campaign in trustee minutes. In any event, the Crash of 1929 soon put an end to such aspirations. The nation experienced bankruptcy on a vast scale, as unemployment exceeded 25 percent and banks failed throughout the country.

At Emory, enrollment fell drastically, to the point that in 1932 one residence hall simply remained locked up. President Harvey Cox announced salary reductions for faculty that year, ranging from 5 to 11 percent, and in 1934 salaries were reduced another 10 percent. Deficits to the budget in some years exceeded 10 percent. Not until 1937–38 did salaries reach their pre-Crash level, including a base salary of thirty-six hundred dollars for full professors.

For Candler the strain was hard. The 1928–29 academic year had brought enrollment to a new high of 129, including seven students in the graduate school who were working principally in theology; the budget for expenditures totaled $69,090, with a deficit of $1,090 (this budget accounted for all salaries, scholarships, general expenses, and administration). The following year, the expenditures remained the same, but the deficit had grown to $2,340 as enrollment slipped to 97. Five years later, in 1934–35, enrollment had dropped further, to 63, while the greatly reduced expenditures of $50,225 included a deficit of $2,225.

In the face of these sinking numbers, Dean Parker nevertheless continued to plead his case for still more support from the university administration and the board of trustees. In his report to President Cox in 1936, he noted,

> [While] the School of Theology has already rendered a splendid service to the church that founded it, . . . it must be prepared to meet the needs of a constantly changing world. Its most vital need is to connect religion with the actual living of the people, rather than to engage in more theoretical discussions about religion. Of course, there should be no looseness of theological conviction, but there should be a more pungent application of the doctrines of Christ.

To help give force to this "pungent application," Dean Parker noted, the school could use a larger library "and other facilities for laboratory investigation of social and religious conditions." More staff and faculty were also necessary to accommodate what, by the end of the decade, would become a larger student body and a large cohort of clergy in the field. From the mid-Depression nadir of 63 students, the enrollment grew to 142 in the fall of 1941, just before the entry of the United States into World War II following Pearl Harbor.

By that time, Dean Parker had retired from the deanship, in 1937. In 1942 he retired from the faculty. His successor as dean would be fully engaged in steering the school through the hazards of war and the challenges of a peacetime boom. 𝒞

*The Theology Building in winter.*

When Franklin Nutting Parker, left, stepped down as dean in 1937, he passed the baton to Henry Burton Trimble, who continued to teach homiletics full time while serving as dean.

## CHAPTER THREE

# "The Immediate Needs Are Plain"

As Candler neared the end of its first quarter-century, the school and the university could look back on a remarkable record of consistent engagement with the church, the academy, and the world.

By the time Franklin Parker participated in his last commencement as dean of the school, in June 1937, Candler had graduated more than 270 bachelors of divinity. Of those, one would write the Emory alma mater, one would write the centennial history of Emory in 1936, one would later become dean of Oxford College, and one would become president of the University of Chicago. Moreover, the Methodist congregation born in the chapel of the theology school in 1920 had grown large enough to merit the expansive and impressive new edifice called Glenn Memorial, dedicated in 1931. Every Candler student was engaged in church work in the Atlanta area by way of required fieldwork. The faculty members were actively recruiting students from nearly every conference of the Methodist Episcopal Church, South, east of the Mississippi. The faculty also was playing an important part in nurturing the future of Methodism in America through participation in the annual and general conferences.

More significantly still, the intellectual energy of the faculty took the school and its aspirant ministers into areas of study that were helping to reshape the culture of the region. Candler's Department of Sociology, for instance, was offering courses in "charities and relief," "the juvenile delinquent," and the "practical sociology" of

Dean Trimble occupied the office originally designated for Chancellor Warren Candler and later used by the director of Pitts Theology Library.

addressing "city problems" and "rural problems." The school's Department of Religious Education already was applying theories of moral development and the psychology of religion, as Candler students learned about ways to tailor religious education specifically for adolescents, college students, and young adults—even to "Teen-Age work in the church." This work in moral development had all the earmarks of the liberal theologians' view that human goodness could be nurtured more surely if one had a thorough grounding in the science of human personality. (This work also foreshadowed, in an interesting though less sophisticated manner, the richer dimensions to come, decades later, through the work of James Fowler and the Center for the Study of Human and Moral Development.) Homiletics courses paid close attention to the use of voice and the lessons of literature for theology, and all students were required to demonstrate proficiency in "the correct use of the English language."

The 1915 bulletin of the theology school had outlined the school's purpose in terms consistent with the aims of an ascendant, liberal American Methodism:

> [Our] educational policy has not been pursued for the achievement of sectarian ends, but for the accomplishment of most pious and patriotic purposes. The object proposed is the promotion of such intellectual culture as will conserve the democratic institutions, social welfare, and religious interests of our country.
>
> The church proposes institutions of learning in harmony with the republican spirit of the American commonwealth and permeated by the principles and influence of the Christian religion.

In terms of the educational uplift and the social transformation of the Southeast, the decade and a half following Dean Parker's resignation would witness a dramatic intensification of Candler's pursuit of these purposes. The fruits of this activity simultaneously met students (and later church members) where they were, while also introducing the broad community of Candler students and interested church supporters to new horizons in theology. Tensions with the church evident in the 1920s subsided. Of more interest was the beginning of the diversification of the faculty. The guiding shepherd who could undertake this process while nurturing a continuing collegiality was a man named Henry Burton Trimble.

Trimble had been reared in Virginia and educated at Roanoke College before earning divinity degrees from Vanderbilt Divinity School and Union Theological

Seminary in New York. He held appointments in half a dozen parishes in Arkansas before making his way back east, all the while developing a reputation for preaching. He was serving a charge in Asheville, North Carolina, in 1931, when Dean Parker recruited him to be professor of homiletics. As Franklin Parker

*In addition to Parker and Trimble, the 1934 Candler faculty shown here include Boone Bowen (Old Testament), Wyatt Aiken Smart (biblical theology), Lavens Thomas (religious education), and William Watkins (church history). Not shown are Professors Horace DuBose (lecturer on archaeology), Andrew Sledd (Greek and New Testament), and William J. Young (professor emeritus of missions).*

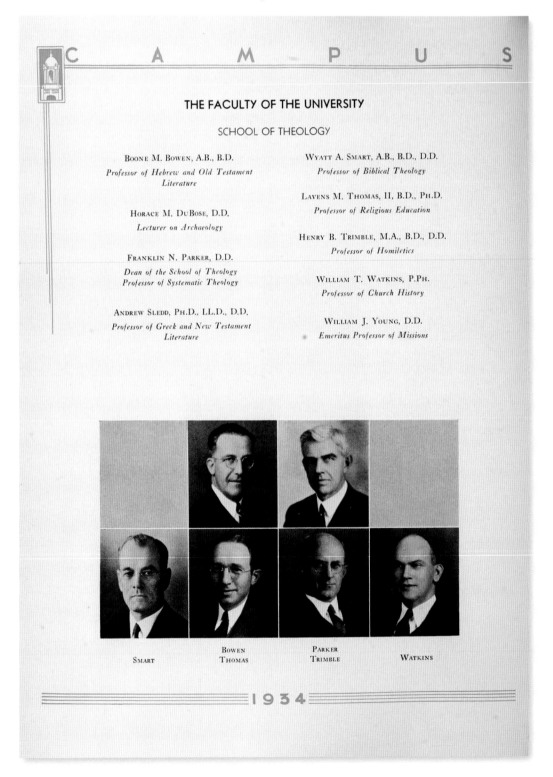

C A M - P U S

**THE FACULTY OF THE UNIVERSITY**

SCHOOL OF THEOLOGY

BOONE M. BOWEN, A.B., B.D.
*Professor of Hebrew and Old Testament Literature*

HORACE M. DuBOSE, D.D.
*Lecturer on Archaeology*

FRANKLIN N. PARKER, D.D.
*Dean of the School of Theology Professor of Systematic Theology*

ANDREW SLEDD, PH.D., LL.D., D.D.
*Professor of Greek and New Testament Literature*

WYATT A. SMART, A.B., B.D., D.D.
*Professor of Biblical Theology*

LAVENS M. THOMAS, II, B.D., PH.D.
*Professor of Religious Education*

HENRY B. TRIMBLE, M.A., B.D., D.D.
*Professor of Homiletics*

WILLIAM T. WATKINS, P.PH.
*Professor of Church History*

WILLIAM J. YOUNG, D.D.
*Emeritus Professor of Missions*

SMART

BOWEN
THOMAS

PARKER
TRIMBLE

WATKINS

1934

resigned from the deanship in 1937, President Harvey Cox turned to Trimble as Parker's replacement. It is not altogether clear why. The faculty of ten included three charter members nearing retirement: Henry Harris, professor of religious education; Wyatt Aiken Smart, professor of Old Testament; and Andrew Sledd, professor of New Testament. Two others—Lavens Matheson Thomas II 24T (religious education) and Boone Bowen (Hebrew and Old Testament literature)— had joined the faculty a year or two before Trimble, and they both had earned the PhD, while Trimble had not. Thomas had gone on from his undergraduate days at Emory to earn a PhD at Yale, and he had distinguished himself at Candler by helping to launch the school's first fieldwork program as well as the annual Ministers' Week, which would become a staple of continuing education for clergy and laity throughout the Southeast for decades to come. Bowen distinguished himself as a teacher by demanding a lot of his students, but he published little as a scholar—one brief paper on the concept of immortality in the Old Testament before the Babylonian exile, and his Yale dissertation on the Hebrew word *chesed* (loving-kindness). It may be that the peculiar combination of abilities necessary for the job at that time presented itself most clearly in Burton Trimble. Although the nation's economy had begun to climb out of the ditch by 1937, the times remained perilous for an academic enterprise, particularly one so young and poorly endowed. The task of administering a theology school called for an extraordinary combination of financial acumen, devotion to the church, and academic experience. In any case, Trimble would prove himself worthy of the trust.

From the beginning, Trimble found the financial challenges of the seminary large but undaunting. In his first annual report, he wrote,

> *The opportunity of the Candler School of Theology is very challenging. It is now definitely looked to to furnish the trained leadership for the Methodist Church of the southeastern part of the United States, a church of nearly two million members. In the light of the increasing importance of this area in the life of the nation, and the religious significance of Methodism to this section, the Candler School of Theology is challenged as are few other theological schools in the world.*
>
> *To meet its obligations the Candler School of Theology must develop in stride with the University as a whole. . . . The immediate needs are plain. The growing service of the School to the Church must begin to lag*

*in the very near future unless the financial resources are substantially increased through endowment or otherwise.*

While the Depression and, later, the war years offered little budgetary space for innovative programming, expansion, or much else besides trying to hold the operation together, the period did demand the kind of pastoral instincts that the Candler School of Theology was trying to hone in its students. These were instincts that Trimble himself possessed, and for which he was often remembered afterward with affection. In Boone Bowen's account, for instance, the bombing of Pearl Harbor on December 7, 1941, led within three weeks to the arrest of a Candler student—Tatsumasa Shirakawa, a native of Japan. A January 29, 1942, memorandum from the Justice Department to J. Edgar Hoover lists Shirakawa as one of a group of "alien enemies" apprehended by presidential warrant. The FBI held him at Fort McPherson, in Atlanta, along with other enemy aliens awaiting repatriation. Through Trimble's intervention, Shirakawa was released into the dean's care and allowed to finish the spring quarter before returning to his homeland and returned to Candler after the war to complete his degree. Other stories of Trimble's personal investment in the welfare of the community—some of them with no relation to Emory or Candler—suggest a man whose preaching demonstrated its conviction through clear and effective acts of faith.

Even as Trimble took office as dean, it was evident that a second European war was on its way. The prospect of another such catastrophe, following the devastation of World War I, agitated the churches in America, and seminary faculties often took the lead in advocating a pacifist approach to international conflict. But as Germany and Japan launched attacks on their respective continents in 1939, prominent American theologians like Reinhold Niebuhr changed their thinking and found reasons to set aside their pacifism. Tellingly, where the faculty at Candler stood in this debate is unclear. Perhaps their focus on preparing ministers for the church inclined them to think of training military chaplains rather than debating just-war theory or the merits of pacifism.

Nor is it clear whether the exemptions in the Selective Service Act for students preparing for ministry did much to maintain enrollment levels through the war years. In his report to President Goodrich White in 1943, Trimble noted that the draft had put downward pressure on admissions. Quite apart from the draft, the urge to enlist propelled many young men into military service, and fully half of the school's forty-eight bachelor of divinity graduates that year sought

**CANDLER CASUALTIES IN WORLD WAR II**   Emory University—and the Candler School of Theology—felt the impact of World War II in personal as well as institutional ways. Among the alumni killed were Goodrich C. White Jr., son of the president of Emory and a graduate of the college. Candler also experienced the loss of two alumni who had entered the military chaplaincy—Hoke S. Bell 34C 36T (shown at right) and Ben R. W. Knowles 37C 39T.

Bell, killed while trying to rescue a wounded soldier, had written to President White just the week before news of his death arrived on campus:

> *Somewhere in Africa*
>
> *March 26, 1943*
>
> *Dear Dr. White:*
>
> *At the time I was stumbling through Emory, I failed her in so many ways that I thought she was doing little for me. But hardly a day passes now but that I bow down in my heart in grateful remembrance of the good things that even I could not escape at Emory. She taught me to not only be unafraid of truth, but to welcome it and enjoy it enough to search for it; to be humble and quiet in the presence of one who knows more than I do, on any subject; to be able to read and enjoy good books in many fields; to believe that the world can be good and beautiful not only in spite of, but partly because of, suffering. . . . The heritage is priceless. I cannot help but be grateful.*
>
> *I have no right to be optimistic concerning the future; but I must reverently and gratefully say here and now, in the midst of shells and fox holes, life has never been so meaningful, and therefore so worth living, as before. . . . A great number of soldiers are thoughtfully rearranging their system of values.*
>
> *Hoke S. Bell*

Elsewhere in the world, another Candler graduate was doing his best to minister to members of his Methodist congregation as war came to their homeland. Kiyoshi Tanimoto 40T, had returned to his native Japan following graduation from Candler, and he was serving a Methodist church in Hiroshima when the atomic bomb was dropped on that city on August 6, 1945. Two miles from ground zero, he was unhurt, but his church was destroyed and his congregation lost 680 of its 800 members. Tanimoto would find in this experience the mission that would occupy much of the rest of his life. In addition to continuing to serve Methodist churches in Japan, he founded the Hiroshima Peace Center Foundation and spoke widely in the United States and elsewhere in behalf of nuclear disarmament. Invited to Emory in December 1986 to receive an honorary doctorate at the convocation celebrating the sesquicentennial of the university, he unfortunately died three months before his scheduled return to the campus. His widow accepted the degree in his memory.

positions as navy chaplains. (In fact, Candler would provide 5 percent of the navy's chaplaincy class of one hundred members that year.)

The close of World War II brought enormous challenges to Emory, but perhaps no college or school at the university felt those challenges as keenly as Candler. The administration had begun to prepare the trustees to meet the needs of a new day as early as 1944, when Dean Trimble reported that the faculty had undertaken to plan "a long-time program of development" aimed at increasing support from the church, appealing to specific individuals for gifts, and building the endowment of the school. That same year, President White persuaded the trustees to launch the first fully organized development office at the university with the aim of laying the foundation for Emory to become a truly great university. "The time is here for us to move forward aggressively in the development of a University in the true sense of the term," he said. This effort meant, to him, not achieving "bigness" but clarifying purpose, building

*Kiyoshi Tanimoto graduated from Candler in 1940 and was serving a church in Hiroshima when the atomic bomb was dropped. Tanimoto returned to Emory at least once, in 1949, for Ministers' Week. At the right is his eyewitness account of Hiroshima in 1945.*

### HIROSHIMA, August 6, 8:15 a.m.
#### 1945
#### an eye-witness account by REV. KIYOSHI TANIMOTO
#### Methodist Pastor in Hiroshima
†

*The address reproduced here was given by the Rev. Kiyoshi Tanimoto, an ordained Methodist Minister, at the eleven o'clock lecture hour at "Ministers' Week", Emory University, Candler School of Theology, Atlanta Ga. The date of delivery: Tuesday, Jan. 18, 1949. This is a transcript of a recording of his address.*

†

I happened to be in the city of Hiroshima at the time of the atomic bomb. It was August 6, 8:15am that the world's first atomic bomb was dropped. I passed by the Central Post Office, what is supposed to be the center of the explosion, about 30 minutes before that catastrophe, so, I saw the city's condition quite well. I went through the city and reached the western edge of it. When I arrived there I saw the flash. I was behind a hill standing in the valley in front of a house. The flash ran suddenly from the east to the west. I took a couple of steps into the garden to lie down on the ground between two rocks and then felt a strong blast of wind. When I got up, the house behind me was destroyed and the concrete wall standing at the entrance was turned over. I saw few people appearing from under the debris. An old woman appeared before me saying, "I'm hurt! I'm hurt!" She was bleeding from her head. I took her to the first aid station 3 blocks away and there I saw many more injured people.

I was so surprised! Up until that time Hiroshima was bombed by B-29s with small shells and just 10 people had been killed, but this time so many were injured. Yet I did not hear an explosion! As a matter of fact there was a tremendous explosion. My mother-in-law lived in a village 25 miles away from Hiroshima and they heard a tremendous explosion, much greater than that which was heard in another town about 5 miles away from this place. But we, inside the city, couldn't hear a sound, yet selectively, improving quality, and increasing effectiveness in meeting the needs of the region and the nation. To achieve these goals, he said, would require a lot more money.

Money was forthcoming to Emory and to many American universities, in the form of direct support of research by the federal government and indirect support of education through tuition grants and guaranteed loans. Little of this money, however, flowed to Candler or to any other theology school because of First Amendment issues. While universities in general, and Emory in particular, became somewhat better off after the war—faculties growing, salaries rising, administrators and staff being added—the theology school had a hard time keeping pace.

Other stresses bore down on Candler. If the experience of war had led hundreds of thousands of servicemen and -women to examine their systems of value, the G.I. Bill made it possible for them to pursue that examination formally at theological schools and to carry their faith into ministry. Between the last prewar year (1940-41) and the first postwar year (1945-46), enrollment at Candler doubled. What's more, the new demography of the student body brought needs that the prewar student body had not had. Unlike the vast majority of the students in Candler's first two decades, who were young bachelors intent on finishing their schooling before marriage, many of the new students at Candler were married, and some of them had children. Suddenly—as at other seminaries around the country—housing issues took on new dimensions, as did campus life, with the growing presence of women (whether as spouses or as religious education students) requiring the seminaries to adapt to still more dramatic changes. In 1946, with the seminary bursting at the seams, Trimble reported that enrollment would have been higher but for the absence of housing, and he proposed construction of a building with forty-eight units for married students and another with fifty units for unmarried students. In time these would be opened as Gilbert Hall and Wesley (later Trimble) Hall.

The war and its aftermath brought a further professionalization of ministry. The military had required that chaplains be graduates of both college and an accredited seminary, and this requirement led the American Association of Theological Schools in various ways to push for recognition of this seven-year academic track as the basic curriculum for a properly trained clergy. The further segmentation of ministry into specialties like the chaplaincy became evident as the curriculum at Candler diversified after the war. One instance was the

appointment of Earl D. C. Brewer as instructor in rural sociology in 1945. Brewer would eventually supervise a broad-ranging, foundation-supported study of religion in the Appalachian region, and throughout his career he focused on preparing ministers for the specialized work in town and country parishes. The addition of this focus to the curriculum not only demonstrated an awareness of the importance of small-town and rural ministry to Methodism in the Southeast but also signaled a heightened attention to the ways in which such ministry might be different from ministry in the cities and suburbs. New courses were offered in clinical pastoral training at Grady Memorial Hospital and in prisons. These clinical courses would persist for only a few years, but they laid the foundation for later and more substantial developments in supervised ministry and, in time, contextual education.

During the 1940s the full curriculum also underwent various modifications that students of the early twenty-first century would recognize. All ministerial knowledge, essentially, was parceled into four areas—the Bible (Old and New Testaments plus biblical theology); expansion of the church (history and missions); thought and life of the religious world (theology, ethics, philosophy, psychology); and the church at work (homiletics, education, sociology, speech, and music). This arrangement closely resembled a plan instituted shortly after the war at Perkins School of Theology at Southern Methodist, the sister university of Emory. Few of the courses offered in the curriculum would sound surprising today: Genesis, Job, Psalms, Isaiah, historical geography, and the history of Israel predominated in Old Testament studies, usually with attention to historical and form critical methods; New Testament courses dealt with the "Synoptic Problem" and offered linguistic and literary analysis of John and the Pauline letters; the Department of Homiletics and Pastoral Theology offered a course in "pastoral efficiency and administration," with particular attention to the "sources of power in the pastor's life and labor," including "a study of some eminently successful pastors."

More interestingly, perhaps, the offerings in systematic theology began turning toward more varied sources of thought than Wesley, Luther, Calvin, and Augustine and the doctrines of the creeds. Mack B. Stokes, appointed to the faculty in 1941, brought a grounding in the personalism of Boston University and began applying this philosophy to theology. He also began teaching a survey of "interpretations of history," with particular attention to Hegel, Marx, Spengler, Berdyaev, and Tillich. In a separate course he introduced his students to "contemporary criticisms of Christianity" found in natural science, psychology, sociology, and philosophy. In some ways this course simply updated the old apologetics of the nineteenth century, but it broadened the discussion of theology in the school, and it exposed neophyte ministers to the kinds of questions they no doubt would encounter in their parishes.

While the curriculum underwent influential modifications in subject and

*Carol N. Huang (left) and Lois M. Hwang (right), shown in the 1948* Campus *yearbook, represented the international reach of Candler and Emory into Asia.*

organization, perhaps no change to the curriculum had as significant a practical impact on the lives of the students as the adjustment of days on which classes were held. From the founding of the school until 1948, classes met Tuesdays through Saturdays on the quarter system. Many students served churches at the same time they were enrolled, so the day between Sunday and the first day of classes on Tuesday presumably gave them time to shift gears from ministry to study. (How they managed the transition in the other direction, between Saturday classes and Sunday services, one can only guess.) In 1948, however, the faculty voted to drop Saturday classes to allow students more time for study and created a four-day week that has largely persisted to the present, with the exception that classes began to be held on Monday afternoons in the 1980s.

The postwar boom in enrollment brought other pressures to the curriculum, especially in the area of fieldwork. This had been required of students since 1937, when Professors Emmett Johnson and Lavens Thomas 24T began building on their experience in teaching courses in religious education. Fieldwork was the beginning of a kind of structured, supervised activity, blending academic and practical training in local settings, that in time would become a hallmark of Candler in its Supervised Ministry and Contextual Education programs. Good Methodists to the core, and committed to the connectionalism of Methodism, Professors Johnson and Thomas organized supervised fieldwork through the contrivance of the "Emory Annual Conference," in which Thomas became the "bishop" and each student was assigned membership in a "district" named for a prominent early Methodist leader. The districts served principally as a kind of administrative overlay to the real conferences and districts where students did their fieldwork, while supervision was the responsibility of the local clergy

*Visitors take in the latest broadcasting technology at the 1955 dedication of the Protestant Radio and Television Center on the Emory campus. The facility was razed after the center moved to more up-to-date quarters in downtown Atlanta in 2001.*

where the students served. This artificial Methodist conference structure at the seminary looked and felt familiar to the students—who for most of this time were all Methodists—and it gave them further experience with the connectional system in which they would be working.

By 1946, however, this decade-old structure appeared to be less and less viable. The student body was older and included many veterans. The students were also far more mobile, driving sometimes long distances to serve parishes that provided not only field experience but also, sometimes more importantly, necessary income. Supervising clergy in the field had other duties and higher priorities than looking out for seminary students, and the tripling of the student body meant stretching the supervisors' time even further as additional students needed attention. In response to these challenges, the faculty adopted a system of practicums and projects that brought the analysis and discussion of field experiences into the classroom, where the faculty began to assume a greater role in mentoring nascent pastors. This approach would flower into a more rigorous supervised ministry during the administration of James T. Laney in the 1970s.

Fieldwork was merely one way in which Candler, under Trimble's guidance, sought to shape and gauge a student's fitness for ministry. Finding the requisite balance between theological acumen and pastoral spirit—or even simply the

**PROTESTANT RADIO AND TELEVISION CENTER** As radio became an increasingly prevalent medium of communication through the 1930s, the church adapted the technology to its work of spreading good news and nurturing souls wherever they could be reached. In the early 1940s, Southern Baptists, Methodists, and Presbyterians held discussions to expand their respective efforts in various southern states, and from these conversations grew *The Protestant Hour*, perhaps the single most enduring and far-reaching effort of mainline Protestant denominations in the realm of broadcasting. First aired on eleven stations in 1945, the program had its home in Atlanta from the beginning. Not until May 1955, however, did the program have a permanent home, located on Clifton Road with the help of Emory University. Other supporting sponsors included the Presbyterian-related Agnes Scott College and Columbia Theological Seminary, along with the Southeastern Jurisdiction of the Methodist Church and Presbyterian, Lutheran, and Episcopal denominations (the Southern Baptists by then had set off in their own direction on their own airwaves). Dean Trimble served as the first chair of the board of trustees of the center until he stepped down from the deanship.

This facility—the Protestant Radio and Television Center—included recording studios and broadcasting capabilities for both radio and television.

For more than half a century *The Protestant Hour*, broadcast from where Emory Point now stands across from the U.S. Centers for Disease Control and Prevention on Clifton Road, brought some of the finest preaching in America into homes and cars and anywhere else that the radio stations carrying it could reach.

By the 1990s the facility and its equipment had become run-down, and Emory University was eager to buy back the land on which the PRTVC was built. *The Protestant Hour* moved into state-of-the-art recording facilities at All Saints' Episcopal Church in downtown Atlanta in early 2001 and three years later merged with the Episcopal Media Center to form the Alliance for Christian Media.

*The Protestant Hour* changed its name to *Day 1* in 2002 and added a television broadcast to the radio format. The archives of the first fifty years of the program reside at the University of Georgia and constitute, in the words of William Willimon 73T, "the best collection of the homiletical art in America, perhaps anywhere in the world." Bandy Professor of Preaching Thomas G. Long served as honorary chair of the campaign to raise funds for restoring and digitizing the collection, which serves as an unparalleled resource for students of preaching and for students of American Protestant theology of the second half of the twentieth century.

balance between a felt call and the competence to fulfill it—has always been a delicate matter. But as the exploration of psychology and sociology deepened through the twentieth century, and as these forms of knowledge came to have a broader impact on society, the theology school reached for these disciplines as tools in the dance of discernment. In 1953 the school began administering twelve hours of tests to entering students "to reveal," in the words of Boone Bowen, a student's "vocational aptitude, . . . psychological state, and . . . level of cultural attainment." Ultimately the student would have to prevail on academic grounds, and ecclesiastical jurisdictions remained accountable for determining a student's readiness for pulpit and parish. As a tool for vocational guidance, however, these tests reflected a growing national church trend toward identifying, in nontheological ways, the professional criteria for ministry.

Always, it seems, Trimble and the faculty sought ways to bridge the life of the academy and the life of the parish. Trimble took the initiative in recognizing the impact of the rural church in the Southeast (where the 1940 U.S. census showed that 63 percent of the population lived in rural areas), and with the leadership of Professor Brewer, the school in 1945 launched a Town and Country School to provide three-week intensive programs for pastors in rural and small-town churches. Within a year the success of this program led to creation of a parallel School for Urban Ministers, which addressed the changes beginning to be felt in the South as the mobility of the nation brought growth to southern cities. At the same time, Candler launched the School for Accepted Supply Pastors—a summer program for part-time ministers who lacked formal theological training but were serving small congregations that could not support full-time ministers. Finally, the seminary began formal instruction to acquaint directors of religious education with rapid developments in audiovisual technology, radio, television, and film.

The pressing need for greater financial resources grew more and more evident during the early 1950s. Candler had already begun to address these needs in 1945, when, for the first time, it requested and received Emory trustee approval to charge tuition and fees. That year tuition and fees amounted to $100 per quarter (the charge would rise to $175 by 1953). Tuition income could pay for only so much instruction, however. Growing by 1950 to become the third-largest Methodist seminary, Candler then had a student/faculty ratio of 27:1, about twice what the Methodist Church deemed to be suitable (15:1). These figures led the dean to call for a doubling of the faculty. Similarly, although a limited number of scholarships provided free tuition and $500 a year for eleven weeks' worth of work by the students receiving them, the dean noted that several competitor schools provided more munificent scholarships.

In October 1950, to begin addressing these and other financial issues in the theology school, the trustees requested a meeting with the bishops of the Southeastern Jurisdiction to devise "ways and means . . . to adequately meet the problems and possibilities now confronting the School of Theology." The bishops readily agreed, and in December that year a daylong meeting resulted in a plan to be presented to the Southeastern Jurisdictional Council in 1951. The implementation of that plan would go a long way toward meeting the school's needs for the coming decade.

The plan would also mean the end of the Trimble administration. Someone was needed to make sure that the plan succeeded, since it called on the jurisdiction to raise sixty thousand dollars annually for Candler and called on the school to raise an additional thirty thousand dollars a year—quite sizable sums of money in those days. The dean had proven himself imaginative in engaging the larger church to support the School of Theology, and he found President White prevailing on him to step down before Trimble would reach the mandatory faculty retirement age of sixty-eight in December 1953, in order to take on the full-time development work. Ever committed to Candler, and willing to continue in harness for a few more years, Trimble accepted the appointment and successfully served as a development officer for four more years, before the burden of travel became too much and he asked to be relieved.

For the last four years of Burton Trimble's life he served as associate pastor of Saint Mark Methodist (now United Methodist) Church in downtown Atlanta. Following his death, in November 1962, the university renamed Wesley Hall in his honor, and this dormitory, built through his good efforts, served as a residential facility and office space until its demolition in 2012.

This aerial view of the Emory campus in 1955 shows the site where Bishops Hall would take the place of parking spaces and trees behind the Theology Building, below and to the right of the athletics track.

## CHAPTER FOUR

# TOWARD INTERNATIONAL EMINENCE

NOT quite four decades after Southern Methodism had set forth a mission for Candler, that mission began to expand in a way that would bear fruit for the school, for Emory, and for the church at large. Having proven itself as a good school for Methodist preachers in a rapidly changing region of the country, Candler now was ready to undertake work that would move it into the first ranks of theological institutions.

That meant welcoming a different kind of faculty member than those who had launched the school. Over the course of a decade or so, Candler would welcome a cadre of superb and transformative scholar/teachers. But to prepare the way for them, the president of Emory would need to replace the theology dean, who in 1953 was about to retire.

Goodrich C. White had succeeded Harvey Cox as president of Emory in 1942. An Emory alumnus and former dean of the college and the graduate school before being elevated to vice president and then president, White declared to the Emory board of trustees after the end of World War II that if the university were to move into the realm of research institutions, now was the time. By 1948 the board had approved the granting of the PhD in four fields, all in the sciences; degrees in the social sciences and humanities would soon follow. Given the historical linkage of the university with Methodism, the size of the school of theology, and

its complementary relationship with the Emory College Department of Religion, a doctoral program in religion appeared to be a natural step in developing the graduate school.

To build on the groundwork that Dean Trimble had already established, White may have reached for someone he considered not only a likely good judge of scholars but also an administrator who could continue Trimble's work of nurturing constructive bonds between church and seminary. If this was his thinking, White certainly sized up his new dean well.

William Ragsdale Cannon, scion of a distinguished family from Dalton, Georgia, traced his lineage to ancestors who had settled in America before the Revolutionary War. More important in his mind, though, was that his namesake William Cannon had been a member of the Christmas Conference in Baltimore in 1784, when American Methodism organized itself into a denomination. (The twentieth-century Cannon, who became a bishop in 1968, was invited to give the episcopal address at the church's bicentennial observance in 1984—no doubt partly in recognition of his forebear.) Whatever else entertained, engaged, and enraptured him throughout his eighty-one years, nothing obsessed Bill Cannon more than the Methodist Church.

In his autobiography, *A Magnificent Obsession*, Cannon describes several deep loves—his mother, Yale, the Candler School of Theology. None of these, however, surpassed his devotion to the church of Jesus Christ. Responding to an altar call at the age of seven (though, as he recalled later, "twelve years of age is generally reckoned as the average" for such experiences; he was precocious in all things), young Cannon decided he was called to preach. His father built him a pulpit, and he began preaching revivals to his boyhood friends in a bespoke cutaway coat and gray-striped pants.

Something of this approach to church life would persist throughout Cannon's ministry—elevated and elegant, clothed in old forms. He preferred the fiction of Walter Scott over that of Mark Twain; he took his sermon material from patristics more than from Luther or Calvin—and from John Wesley more than from the news of the day; he found Roman Catholicism appealing in its liturgy (and its vestments); and he regretted that a young woman he loved in his college days married someone else, because she was highly educated and fluent in several languages and would have been excellent at cross-referencing his footnotes in Greek and Latin.

All of twenty-six years old when he arrived at Candler in 1943, Cannon was a proud University of Georgia Bulldog who had gone on to become a Yale Bulldog while earning a divinity degree and (in only two years) a doctorate. In 1943 he was the only clergy member of the North Georgia Conference with a PhD, and he had

*Bishops Hall was dedicated in 1957.*

William Ragsdale Cannon served
as dean of Candler from 1953
until his election as bishop of The
United Methodist Church in 1968.

gained a year of experience as minister of Allen Memorial Methodist Church in Oxford, Georgia, the year before coming to Candler.

Cannon took himself seriously, as he demonstrated late in life in the detailed autobiographical account of his election as bishop in 1968—every ballot recalled, every twist of the plot analyzed. His narrative suggests an extreme view of the importance of episcopal electioneering and of the persons who come to the fore by means of it. He also had a sense of humor, however, and could use it at his own expense, as when he recounted his first year as a professor at Candler. He had proudly exercised such high academic standards during his first semester of teaching that all but two of the thirty students in his required course in church history failed the course. At the end of the semester, during Dean Trimble's holiday party, Professor Boone Bowen—who also freely distributed failing grades—congratulated Cannon on having even tougher standards than Bowen's. Dean Trimble, overhearing the remark, publicly commented that these two were congratulating themselves not for high standards but for their own poor pedagogy! It was they who had failed their students in both senses of the word.

Recognizing the truth of the dean's mild scolding, Cannon worked hard to become a better teacher by writing out all of his lectures—and then leaving the lecture texts at home in order to speak from memory. (Indeed, his memory was impressive, as he usually quoted biblical passages while holding his Bible closed against his chest—a theatrical touch possibly meant to impress upon the hearer the importance of learning scripture by heart, but often prompting the silent rejoinder, "Show-off!")

Whatever insecurities Cannon may have felt as a teacher, scholar, and young bachelor on a faculty of married churchmen, he clearly had moved beyond them after a decade at Candler. Returning from a summer trip abroad in 1953, Cannon found that Dean Trimble and President White had settled upon Cannon as the next dean and had recommended the appointment to the board of trustees. (Nolan Bailey Harmon had been White's first choice, but Harmon preferred to remain book editor of the Methodist Church and a trustee of Emory. He would later serve as bishop and, for a quarter of a century after retirement, as a faculty member at Candler.)

Cannon himself never divulged—if he ever knew—why the president chose him over other members of the faculty to serve as dean. Cannon was not the only faculty member with scholarly credentials. Mack Stokes had earned his PhD from Boston University, where he had come under the sway of personalist philosophy and theology, and he brought a wide-ranging philosophical grounding to his work in systematic theology; perhaps it ranged too far. Earl Brewer had proven himself as an innovative sociologist of religion and contributor to the continuing education of clergy, but his field of scholarship may have lain too far outside the mainstream of the curriculum. The other faculty members with doctoral degrees were all relatively new to the faculty: James May had joined the faculty as assistant professor of church administration in 1948; James McConkey Robinson—later to gain prominence as a scholar of the Nag Hammadi library—had arrived as instructor in biblical theology only in 1952; and Frederick Prussner arrived as instructor in Old Testament in the fall of 1953. It may be that the president settled on Cannon because he was the only one of the faculty members with the combination of a Georgia pedigree, an Ivy League education, and expertise in Wesleyan theology.

White may also have been disposed to appoint Cannon as dean because the president had come to know him well during Cannon's time as minister of Allen Memorial Church in Oxford, where White's mother was a member. Cannon regularly ministered to her and conversed with her son during White's monthly visits. A warm personal regard had developed during that year and in Cannon's subsequent years on the faculty. But more than friendship guided the president's choice of Cannon.

The reasons for the precipitate appointment of Cannon as dean may be known only to those long gone. Since the university had a policy of mandatory retirement on the first of September following a faculty member's sixty-eighth birthday, the Candler faculty expected that Dean Trimble would retire in September 1954, after turning sixty-eight the previous December. In both Boone Bowen's account and Cannon's own telling, some aspirational jockeying had begun to jostle the faculty more than a year in advance of Trimble's retirement. Some on the faculty had already written the president to advise that it would be best for the school if an internal candidate were appointed to succeed Trimble. Perhaps it was a desire to cut off the development of factions and later recriminations that led the president to consult with his board chair, Charles Howard Candler Sr., and settle on Cannon. In any event, when White strode into the meeting of the Candler faculty in September 1953, it came as a shock

**NOLAN BAILEY HARMON**     At his death in June 1993 Nolan Bailey Harmon was just a month shy of celebrating his 101st birthday, yet he had been retired for only five years from teaching at the Candler School of Theology. He had been among the first students to walk Emory's Atlanta campus nearly eighty years earlier.

Born in Mississippi in 1892, the son, grandson, and great-grandson of Methodist ministers, Harmon taught school for two years after graduating from Millsaps College. Perhaps responding to the family calling, he enrolled at Candler in the fall of 1916. The new campus had just opened with all of four buildings—the Theology Building, the Law School, and two dormitories. "Theologs," as seminary students were called, were assigned to live in Dobbs Hall; Harmon later recounted that the latches were not all secured on the doors when he moved in, so the doors banged open and shut in the wind all night.

Bishop Nolan Harmon taught at
Candler in retirement until five
years before his death at the
age of 101.

The banging would get worse—not from the doors, but from a clang of doubt prompted by the intense study of scripture and theology. Nearly deciding to give up the ministry as a vocation whose verities he was unsure of, he had almost settled on another career when he had what he later called a "postintellectual conversion." That experience forever removed any doubt about the presence and faithfulness of Christ in his life.

When the United States entered World War I in April 1917, Harmon struggled again, this time with the question of whether to enlist and go to officers' training school. Asking Professor Franklin Parker for advice before heading to Fort McPherson, he heard Parker exclaim, "You are a minister of God, and you have no right to take weapons in your hand to kill with!" In the end, by a circuitous way, Harmon managed to earn special dispensation to be ordained early and join the army chaplaincy. Going to war ended Harmon's Candler experience for nearly half a century.

After the war Harmon earned a master's degree at Princeton and began his parish ministry. Harmon's talents as a writer and editor, however, soon lifted him out of the pulpit and into the realm of books, as he was elected book editor of the newly reunited Methodist Church in 1939. In that capacity he served as general editor of the influential twelve-volume *Interpreter's Bible* and helped to write the liturgy for the new denomination. As the head of Abingdon Press, he edited scholars like Roland Bainton and Georgia Harkness, Stanley Hopper and Leslie Weatherhead.

Besides his position as editor, Harmon had been elected a delegate to every General Conference of his denomination from 1930 to 1956, so his standing in the church was high. It was not surprising, then, when he was elected bishop in 1956, assigned first to the Charlotte, North Carolina, area, and later to Kentucky and (simultaneously) North Alabama. During his second quadrennium as bishop he led a group of prominent clergy in Birmingham, Alabama, to attempt to bring peace to the conflict then raging around the issue of civil rights. On the day that Governor George Wallace blocked the doorway of the University of Alabama in Tuscaloosa rather than allow it to be integrated peacefully, Harmon read a statement of protest against Wallace's action to the Annual Conference over which the bishop was then presiding. As the people of Birmingham voted the Bull Connor police regime out of office in 1963, Harmon gathered in the city with Episcopal and Catholic bishops, Methodist Bishop Paul Hardin of southern Alabama, and the leading rabbi of Alabama to call for a peaceful transition that would allow new city leadership to move forward. Their public statement—which Harmon always defended as "a sensible message"—was the spur to the more famous reply, Martin Luther King Jr.'s "Letter from Birmingham Jail."

Following his retirement in 1964, Harmon turned again to editing and produced *The Encyclopedia of World Methodism*. He also returned to Emory as a visiting professor of practical theology—a position he held for nearly a quarter of a century, until 1988, when flagging energy finally removed him from the classroom. (According to legend, he never gave a grade lower than an A, making him a popular professor, but probably undermining to some degree his own high regard for the intellectual work of the ministry.) Elected to the Emory board of trustees in 1940, he served as an active trustee until 1964 and then continued to attend board meetings as a trustee emeritus almost until his death.

These Candler students in the 1950s included, from left to right: Yeshuo Kobayashi of Japan; Tzetan Litov of Bulgaria; Burton J. Cheng of China; Herbert Manns of Germany; Yu Chi Teng of China; Charles Son of Korea; Hilda Keng of China; and Friedman Rossborg of Norway.

when he announced that Trimble would be moving into a development position, and Cannon would become dean effective immediately.

By the time the graduate school was prepared in 1958 to admit its first PhD candidate in religion, Cannon had made faculty appointments that would shape the direction of the theology school and ensure the success of the Graduate Division of Religion (GDR). Notably Cannon himself made these appointments; they did not follow the path familiar to later generations of academics, who have come to expect search committees, winnowing of résumés, days of interviews, and finally an offer. No—Cannon inquired here and there about a promising academic or a rising young scholar and simply made that prospective faculty member an offer.

In addition to appointing Mack Stokes as associate dean in charge of nurturing the GDR, Cannon recruited E. Clinton Gardner from Yale in the field of social ethics; William Mallard from Duke in church history; Manfred Hoffmann from Heidelberg in church history; Theodore Runyon Jr. from Tübingen in systematic theology; Theodore Weber from Yale in social ethics; and Hendrikus Boers from South Africa in New Testament. These professors would influence generations of divinity and doctoral students, help determine the priorities of the theology school through the next three decades, and reinvigorate the professoriate in religion for the turn of the century.

Besides these faculty members, who demonstrated remarkable staying power, the roster of Cannon's appointments included a number of scholars who left Candler for opportunities elsewhere and gained renown for their later work. These included John B. Cobb Jr. 43Ox, the great process theologian; Robert Funk, the New Testament scholar who helped to found the Jesus Seminar; and Franklin Littell, who, while at Emory, taught the first graduate seminar in America on the Holocaust and later would help to establish the field of Holocaust studies while at Southern Methodist University and Temple University.

Cannon appointed an international faculty, with the addition of scholars from Germany, Great Britain, South Africa, and Israel. He also appointed the first Jewish professor on the Candler faculty: Immanuel Ben-Dor, a native of Israel and a faculty member in the Oriental Institute at the University of Chicago, came to Candler in 1957 as professor of archaeology and semitics, and he served in that role until his retirement and untimely death in 1969.

This faculty, by the end of the 1950s, was carrying Candler into theological realms that would not have been imagined by those 1920s Southern Methodists upset with

modern biblical criticism. It was not that the faculty was so radical. Rather there was a kind of congenial intellectual ferment among the faculty that enlivened the experience of the students as well as the faculty itself. In mid-decade Stokes was teaching Borden Parker Bowne's philosophy of personalism, Robinson was teaching Barth and Bultmann, while Gordon Thompson was exploring "the basis of authority of the evangelical faith" in terms of mysticism, Thomism, existentialism, and rationalism. Runyon was teaching Kierkegaard, Tillich, and Bonhoeffer, while Mallard was teaching courses in Christianity and literature, with attention to Ibsen, O'Neill, Frost, Faulkner, Camus, and Auden, among others. Gardner, whose work at Yale with H. Richard Niebuhr informed so much of his teaching at Candler over four decades, was offering a remarkable range of courses exploring the social dimensions of the Christian faith: a course on Christianity and communism that included readings in Marx, Lenin, Stalin, Khrushchev, and Mao; a course on Christianity and race relations; another on religion and economic life. Weber's Wesleyanism, channeled through a filter of social justice, led him to become for decades Candler's preeminent interpreter of "the social teaching of the Christian churches," beginning with his early courses dealing with natural law, usury, capitalism, slavery, war, sex, the status of women, religious liberty, and social reconstruction.

Although all of these faculty members were Methodists, it was not merely (or even necessarily) their shared denominational affiliation that allowed their divergent perspectives to coexist. Rather it was a sense of collegiality fostered in part by the dean but also in part by a conviction they shared with the school's earlier faculty—a belief that intellect in service to faith could have a transformative impact on the church and society. That conviction led the Candler faculty to play a significant role in one of the great instances of social change in American history.

By the late 1950s the storm brewing around the move toward integration of education in the South was about to break over Atlanta. The 1954 decision by the U.S. Supreme Court in *Brown v. Board of Education* prompted legislation in the Georgia Assembly that mandated the closing of any Georgia public schools that took steps to integrate as a result of *Brown*. In Atlanta a countermovement was under way to defeat this segregationist retrenchment, which was viewed as bad for business, bad for the city's image, and bad for the moral fiber of society. Led by clergy and many others in the religious community, the movement aimed to keep the public schools open at all costs.

On November 3, 1957, the *Atlanta Journal* and the *Atlanta Constitution* published what has come to be known as the "Ministers' Manifesto," signed by eighty white members of the Atlanta Christian Council and calling for moderation, the rule of law, freedom of speech, mutual respect, preservation of the public schools, racial harmony, and prayerful consideration of a way forward. A large fraction of the eighty signatories were alumni of Candler or Emory College. One year later, in November 1958, the Atlanta newspapers published another open letter, this time from more than 350 Emory faculty members and administrators who reiterated the need to keep the schools open. Nearly all of the theology faculty signed the letter.

Even before the issue of race had begun to be fought in public in Atlanta, however, the theology faculty had raised the matter in its own dealings with the university administration. The faculty had thought of developing interseminary collaboration with the Interdenominational Theological Center, the historically black set of institutions near the Atlanta University Center, and Dean Cannon commissioned a committee of three to seek permission from the university president. Earl Brewer, Clinton Gardner, and Theodore Weber met with Robert Whitaker, the president's assistant, who, in Weber's recollection, "stonewalled us the whole time," finally ending the meeting with no conclusion.

*Preaching takes practice, and by 1958 Candler had installed new technology to make the practice and learning from it more efficient.*

In April 1957 Dean Cannon appointed a committee to review the changing mores and legal codes of the nation and to bring forward recommendations about the restrictions around race at Candler and Emory. Drawing on this committee's report and on the 1956 Methodist Discipline, the theology faculty as a whole produced a resolution encouraging the university to review the policies of the school of theology—especially those pertaining to race—with the aim of "making sure that these policies and practices are Christian." Moreover, the faculty voiced their "willingness and readiness to have [black students] as members of our classes and of the student body." The resolution could not have been more clear in its intention to push the university toward integration. Perhaps because of that clarity, the resolution hit a brick wall in the board of trustees, to whom President White presented it with no comment or recommendation. The board simply did not act on it.

One sticking point for Emory, as for other private educational institutions in the state, was certain statutes on the books in Georgia. State law stipulated that any tax-exempt school, college, or university that offered instruction to both "colored" and white students would lose its tax exemption. Curiously, the state had never objected to Candler or Emory enrolling students from Korea, Japan, or China. But the threat of university bankruptcy because of the lost tax exemption was, in the pent-up political divisiveness of the time, quite real, and neither the board nor the administration wanted to push the issue in 1957 or 1958.

Change did come inevitably, however. The way forward was cleared by transitions in the university administration and board leadership. In 1957 President White was succeeded by S. Walter Martin, a well-intentioned but hapless captain, out of his depth in the storm, who lacked the deft hand at the rudder to steer through rough seas. Charles Howard Candler Sr., the board chair, who had stood firm against every initiative toward integration, died just one month after Martin took office, leaving his handpicked president to choose his way as best he could. Candler's successor as board chair, Henry Bowden Sr., a savvy and well-known Atlanta attorney and prominent Methodist layman, began charting a different course for the university through the tempest. Recognizing as others did that Emory would either integrate or lose its momentum toward gaining national stature (loss of faculty, loss of federal funding, loss of prestige), Bowden and the board began laying the groundwork for opening the doors of the university to all qualified students regardless of race. As President Martin prepared to step down in 1962, the university, claiming that the state laws governing tax exemption infringed on academic freedom, brought suit against the state of Georgia to invalidate the statutes. After losing in superior court, the university carried its fight to the Georgia Supreme Court, which agreed with Emory in September 1962. The way was open, and Candler faculty and alumni helped to open it.

As Boone Bowen noted in his 1972 history of the school of theology,

> *During the Parker administration barriers against women had been removed. In the Trimble era discrimination against non-Methodists had been discontinued. The Cannon administration witnessed the elimination of racial discrimination. Candler was at last free to admit or reject a student solely on the grounds of . . . academic and moral qualifications.*

As an administrator Cannon continued many of the imaginative initiatives of his predecessor. Trimble had proposed creating an advisory body whose members would serve as ambassadors between the seminary and the church. Under Cannon's leadership this body took shape as the Committee of One Hundred. Trimble also had proposed the One Percent Plan, through which churches served by graduates of Candler could voluntarily designate 1 percent of their budgets to support the school. In time Cannon would argue that this program should include Duke Divinity School, and that the 1 percent donations should come not just from the churches of Candler graduates but from all churches in the Southeastern Jurisdiction of the Methodist Church. Although the Committee of One Hundred and the university trustees initially thought that inviting Duke to share the pie was folly, the significant

**OTIS TURNER** Candler's first African American student was Otis Turner (shown here with the Candler student government in 1968), a graduate of Albany State University and a former Peace Corps volunteer, who enrolled as a divinity student in 1965. After receiving his divinity degree in 1969, Turner earned a PhD in social ethics from Emory's Graduate Division of Religion. Turner went on to teach for a time at Wofford College and had a long career as a minister in the Presbyterian Church (USA), developing policies for racial justice on behalf of that denomination.

increase in revenues from the jurisdiction-wide offerings more than offset any loss from having to share with Duke, and in time the program was expanded to include the entire United Methodist Church as a way of funding all of its seminaries through the Ministerial Education Fund of the Board of Higher Education and Ministry.

With regard to finances in general, Cannon recalled that his "method in proposing a budget was to underestimate income and overestimate expenses." He may have thought of himself as uniquely clever in this approach, but it has been a ploy of deans for generations in countless schools and universities, in order to safeguard themselves from the difficult decisions about when and where to determine priorities.

Although he was the first dean of Candler to have earned a PhD, and later would be called the "scholar bishop" because of his output of books, Cannon was not a seminal or even a particularly good scholar in the view of some of his faculty. Still, as one of his colleagues would later put it, he had a "strong logical mind," and he put it to use in addressing many of the critical moments that came along during his fifteen years as dean. The most memorable of these critical moments occurred just two years before the end of Cannon's deanship.

In the fall of 1965, as the Emory board of trustees was preparing to announce the beginning of a major fund-raising campaign, *Time* magazine ran a story about a small group of American theologians whose scholarly work combined interest in Kierkegaard, Bonhoeffer, and Nietzsche with a radical interpretation of the incarnation, crucifixion, and resurrection of Christ that carried these theological doctrines to their logical extreme. Among the theologians was an associate professor in the Department of Religion in Emory College—Thomas Jonathan Jackson Altizer (named for his ancestor, "Stonewall" Jackson).

Reaction to the article was swift and largely hostile to the theologians. Perhaps recognizing the potential for stoking a good controversy and increasing sales, the magazine expanded the story for its issue published the week before Easter of 1966. The red-framed cover of *Time* stunned readers with a question in large red letters printed on a black background: "Is God Dead?"

At Emory the president's office was soon besieged by phone callers and letter writers seeking Altizer's dismissal. To their credit, both President Sanford Atwood (a Presbyterian) and Board Chair Henry Bowden (a Methodist) defended the academic freedom of the scholar Altizer to publish his best thinking about his subject. There was never a question at Emory whether Altizer would remain on the faculty; of course he would. Legend has it that even the Coca-Cola magnate Robert Woodruff, the greatest benefactor to Emory in the second half of the twentieth century, inserted

**COMMITTEE OF ONE HUNDRED**     As early as the spring of 1949, Dean Burton Trimble had put together a Theological Advisory Committee comprising fifty-eight laypersons and clergy from throughout the Southeastern Jurisdiction, with the aim of spreading the responsibility and joy of raising funds for the theology school. The initiative went nowhere.

Still, recognizing the potential of dedicated church members and Candler alumni to foster support of the school, he tried again in April 1953 and invited a number of prominent and influential Methodist laymen to a conversation. These included Henry Bowden, chair of the Emory board of trustees, and D. W. Brooks 64H—CEO of GoldKist, an Emory trustee, and an agricultural advisor to several U.S. presidents. Over the next four months, with either Bowden or Brooks or both in tow, Trimble traveled the Southeast to meet with Methodist church members who were successful business leaders and professionals, and he enlisted their support for the idea of building a cohort of committed ambassadors in behalf of the university and the theology school. Their role would be to help interpret the academy to the church, generate goodwill among the churches, and ultimately encourage financial commitments to Candler. In September that year the bishops of the jurisdiction met on the Emory campus, heard Trimble's pitch in behalf of the new organization, and gave it their blessing. The Committee of One Hundred was born.

It would be a number of years before the committee actually numbered one hundred. (Records suggest that the milestone was passed in 1967, though it may have been earlier.) Through the years, the Committee of One Hundred has played a vital role in fostering understanding and strong ties between the school and the churches it seeks to serve. Some of the committee's members have gone on to become university trustees; most have continued to make significant personal contributions to Candler long after their formal term of service has ended. Of all the advisory bodies for the various schools and colleges at Emory, the Committee of One Hundred has proven to be perhaps the most active, and certainly the most effective in fulfilling its mandate.

D. W. Brooks (left center of table) and Henry Bowden (right center) provided the driving force to launch the Committee of One Hundred.

**BISHOPS HALL** When Candler occupied its building on the Emory University Quadrangle in 1916, the school had ample space for teaching the 134 students enrolled that year, for housing offices for the eight faculty members, and for shelving the several thousand volumes in the library. Candler had so much space, in fact, that there was room for a chapel whose marble-clad interior walls could accommodate the whole school community and then some.

By 1954, however, enrollment was approaching 500 students, the faculty had grown to fifteen (including the dean, who taught a full load), and the library had expanded into both wings of the basement. (There had been some relief when the Asa Candler Library was built on the east end of the Quadrangle, enabling the move of the library serving Emory College from under the chapel to the new building; the space under the chapel was converted to offices.)

Dean Cannon and President Goodrich White invited the bishops of the Southeastern Jurisdiction to campus for a meeting in 1954, and they presented the bishops with the urgency of erecting a second building for the theology school. The new structure would cost $600,000, the bishops learned, and another $150,000 would be required to renovate the old Theology Building. To their credit, the bishops rose to the challenge and set about stumping for their respective shares of the necessary funds in their episcopal areas.

In January 1957 the school broke ground for a building to the north of its original home, and construction proceeded so quickly that the new quarters were ready for dedication on September 20. Named Bishops Hall to honor those who had led in raising most of the funds, the new structure was celebrated by a daylong series of events including a special convocation on theological education in the morning, the consecration of Bishops Hall in the afternoon, and a dinner for the College of Bishops and the Committee of One Hundred in the evening. Ten bishops of the Southeastern Jurisdiction (seven active and three retired) received honorary degrees from Emory during the consecration ceremony.

For another half-century this building withstood remarkable vicissitudes as the university campus changed around it. White Hall and the Atwood Chemistry Center erupted like ugly blisters to its west; Cannon Chapel rose between Bishops Hall and Pitts Library; a giant chiller turbine was planted to the east; parking around the building was whittled to nothing; and at last a brand-new edifice, the Rita Anne Rollins Building, opened in 2008 as a sign that the days of Bishops Hall were numbered. Its dismantling occurred in the spring of 2013.

In the meanwhile, some six thousand seminary students passed through the portals of Bishops Hall before the last chunk of its stucco was removed to make way for a new library in time for the school's centennial.

himself in the issue and called the president to say that if Altizer were canned, Emory would not receive another dime from the philanthropist or his foundation. No record of the phone call has so far been found.

Naturally, however, since the controversy centered on theology, a great swath of readers of *Time* assumed that the school of theology at Emory should be

the target of their ire, and the dean of theology felt compelled to respond. From Cannon's own account of the episode, in *A Magnificent Obsession*, one can surmise that he did not fully understand the sophisticated theology behind the school of thought that Altizer represented. (Nor, in fact, did most of those who reacted in outrage and despair.) What Cannon did understand was the need to defend Altizer's academic freedom. As President Atwood and the board of trustees delayed in making any public response to the outcry over Altizer's place at this Methodist university, Cannon dictated a fourteen-hundred-word statement that he asked his secretary to type up, and he sent it to Atwood for review. Atwood shared it that afternoon with the faculty of the undergraduate Emory College in a previously scheduled meeting, and at the urging of both the president and the faculty, Cannon sent the statement to the Atlanta newspapers.

Making clear that Altizer was neither a member of the Candler faculty (and thus not liable to sanction of any kind from the theology dean) nor a member of ecclesiastical orders (especially, need it be said, the Methodist Church), Cannon went on to issue a defense of not only academic freedom but religious freedom as well. Only through such freedom, he emphasized, can human rights and truth be served. What is more, he continued—church historian that he was—the history of the church itself demonstrates that theological controversy is often the way forward: the doctrine of the Trinity arose out of the Arian debates of the fourth century; the Reformation issued

*Among the ever-flowing stream of distinguished visitors from various theological perspectives was Norman Vincent Peale, shown here at a Key Laymen's Conference at Candler in 1967.*

from abuses of the sixteenth century; Methodist evangelism itself was controversial as a response to the bland deism of the eighteenth century. Finally, he concluded, "God is not dead at Emory. He is very much alive in the teaching and leadership of this great Christian university. We are big enough to absorb and use all forms of opinion."

For a time, Altizer was a theological rock star of sorts, making the rounds of talk shows and lecturing throughout the country. (These events did not always end well, as he had to make a hurried exit from the *Merv Griffin Show* while the audience chanted for Altizer's death.) At Emory, Mack Stokes debated Altizer in a public forum in the Alumni Memorial University Center. Stokes later recounted that the debate—and Emory's determination to hold it—"cleared the atmosphere."

By odd coincidence, Altizer left Emory the same year that Dean Cannon left Candler. In 1968, as Cannon was elected bishop, Altizer accepted appointment to the Department of English at the State University of New York at Stony Brook, where he eventually retired.

It would be a mistake to assume that Candler—and Cannon—weathered the "death of God" storm with complete grace. Although Cannon could not touch Altizer, one faculty member who felt the sting of the dean's orthodoxy was William Mallard. In response to the initial *Time* article of October 1965, Mallard had sent a letter to the editor defending the intellectual integrity of Altizer, who was both a colleague in the Graduate Division of Religion and a friend. Following the 1966 cover story, the controversy was picked up by Ralph McGill, the famous editor and later publisher of the *Atlanta Constitution*. Regarded as a beacon of sanity and progressiveness on racial matters, McGill showed little tolerance for what he called "theological morticians" in an editorial he wrote lambasting Altizer and company. Again, Mallard wrote to the editor, this time not only defending Altizer's integrity but also suggesting that the approach of the "death of God" theologians had some theological merit. Mallard wrote,

> *Theology has almost always progressed by taking the content of the contemporary sensibility (pagan and damning though it may seem!) and somehow grasping its real truth, yet within the perspective of the New Testament. A classic example is Thomas Aquinas. How the Church trembled over the threat of that old scientific pagan, Aristotle! Yet Thomas embraced the Philosopher, keeping the integrity of Aristotle's thought, but shrewdly weaving it into the fabric of the Christian confession. So Altizer has gone the full route with the atheistic nihilists. He knows the integrity of the modern pagan cry, "God is dead." Yet,*

*as a Christian, he has grasped that experience within the New Testament dimensions. The death of God was sealed at the cross, in Jesus, and looked forward to the resurrection of an entirely new God-man relationship, which we are now just really beginning to grasp and appreciate. I find this full of rich possibility—that we have a chance to do for our century something of what Thomas did for his.*

The next year, 1967, Mallard published an essay in *Toward a New Christianity: Readings in the Death of God Theology.* This collection of diverse essays, edited by Altizer, included authors from John Updike (writing about Kierkegaard) to John B. Cobb Jr. (writing about crisis theology and postmodernism) to such theological eminences as Barth, Buber, Tillich, and Bultmann. Mallard's own essay followed several by Altizer and his like-minded theologians Paul van Buren and William Hamilton.

Calling his essay "A Perspective for Current Theological Conversations," Mallard wrote what appears to be, nearly half a century afterward, an uncontroversial elaboration of the bases of Christian belief in God, Jesus Christ, the resurrection, and the church as the body of Christ. Perhaps the simple inclusion of the essay in a book titled *Toward a New Christianity* caught the dean's attention (what was wrong with the old Christianity?). Perhaps the editors' introductory paragraph to Mallard's essay troubled him (Mallard "would seem to be the only radical theologian who at present is capable of speaking from within the church, just as he is the only radical who speaks as a historian"). Did the dean really want a radical theologian on his faculty?

The question was crucial, in its literal etymological sense: it went to the crux of things; it was a matter of the cross and its meaning. Before long Mallard was required to submit a written statement of his theological views for consideration by the dean and the full professors of the school. As Mallard recalled later, he then met with this body for some six hours to determine whether his theological position had an acceptable place at Candler. In the end, the faculty concluded that, indeed, he and his theology did belong at Candler. Whatever Mallard felt about this inquisition at the time, he later came to believe that the senior faculty's acceptance of his theological statement indicated "that the school was genuinely open to a variety of approaches, interests, and concerns respecting the academic exploration of theology and associated disciplines."

*When Emory University created its first endowed professorships, in 1960, with a bequest from its late board chair Charles Howard Candler Sr., the twenty professors named to the positions included at least one faculty member from each school. G. Ray Jordan, professor of homiletics at Candler, had joined the faculty in 1945. During his career he published 17 books, more than 200 articles, and some 250 book reviews. Ranked among the best preachers in the country at the time, Jordan also served as a member of the Peace Commission of the Methodist Church.*

In fact, Cannon might have had concern about more than Mallard. According to Altizer's recollection, published forty years after the furor, his thinking took much inspiration from work that was being done among Cannon's own faculty. It was at Emory, he says,

> where I came under the impact of Walter Strauss, Gregor Sebba, and John Cobb, and also under the impact of the New Testament scholars William Beardslee, James Robinson, Robert Funk, Norman Perrin, and Hendrik Boers, all of whom became progressively radical while at Emory. It was as though Emory was a truly radical center, or surely it was so theologically. Such an environment would be impossible to imagine today, but that was a time of breakthrough theologically.

When Cannon was elected bishop in 1968, it was, by his own account, the fulfillment of an ambition that was not an ambition. That is, although the episcopal office appears to have drawn him from early on, as the perfect role in which to realize his gifts of preaching, pastoral ministry, and administration, he recognized the degree to which attaining it would depend on the will of the people—or the will of God. His autobiography recounts with astonishing detail the balloting that took place both in 1964—when he narrowly lost election—and in 1968, when he finally won his place.

Most tellingly, he recounts in his autobiography his apparent anguish—softened by humor—over the possibility that his status as a lifelong bachelor might diminish his chances to become bishop. Told that unmarried men were rarely elected as bishops, and that it would help his chances to be married, he responded, "What if I marry and am not elected anyway? What will I do with a wife?" When, at last, he was able to wear the scarlet clerical blouse, he almost crowed that he had not had to marry after all.

As a bishop he continued to serve Candler and Emory through membership on the board of trustees, where his seniority in episcopal office eventually led to his serving as vice chair. His friendship with Jimmy Carter—at whose presidential inauguration he had offered the invocation—provided the entrée for the university to invite Carter to become the first U.S. president to visit the Emory campus. Carter spoke and turned a shovel of dirt at the ceremonial ground-breaking for Cannon Chapel in August 1979. The chapel bears Cannon's name partly as a lever for raising funds from the Methodist Church in the Southeast, but largely in tribute to his contributions to the church and school of theology.

The achievements of the theology school during the Cannon administration set in motion the transition of the school toward greatness. (The full transition would require the work of at least two more deans.) Cannon's delegation of responsibility for graduate study through the appointment of Mack Stokes as director of the Graduate Division of Religion set a firm foundation for building an eminent program in the study of religion. Cannon's personal style and devotion to the church as both an earnest believer and a career organization man earned him the confidence of bishops and lay leaders and enabled him to secure funding for Bishops Hall, establish the Committee of One Hundred, and create the One Percent Plan as a lasting stream of income from the churches to the seminary. Despite some missteps, he generally fostered a spirit of collegiality among the faculty (exemplified by his own close friendship with Mack Stokes, whose theology differed from his own) and permitted a variety of theological positions to engage with each other constructively. Blessed with the boom years of theological education in America, which coincided with national material security and spiritual reawakening, Cannon also took advantage of the times. He was doubly fortunate in being elected as a bishop just before the end of the sixties, as the spirit of the age would bring true radical transformation to Candler. 

From its beginning, Candler has made a central role for worship as a place that forms and expresses its life as a community.

*Landscaping in front of the Theology Building has changed over the years.*

## CHAPTER FIVE

# WOMEN AT CANDLER

BISHOP Warren Candler opposed many things. Some were certainly evil—lynching, for one—while others were debatable then as now: intercollegiate athletics, the unification of northern and southern Methodism, and partaking of alcohol. Among the bishop's fast-held prejudices that time and enlightenment have left in the dustbin of history, his opposition to coeducation stands foremost.

As chancellor of the new university in Atlanta, Candler communicated regularly to the board of trustees from 1915 until stepping down in 1920, and his "Chancellor's Report" for two board meetings set forth the reasoning for his stance against coeducation. In the minutes for June 8, 1918, the bishop goes on record about the admission of Eléonore Raoul to the law school; she was the first woman ever enrolled at Emory. Legend has it that the previous fall she had seized on the opportunity presented by the chancellor's absence from campus and had knocked on the door of the agreeable law dean, Sam Cole Williams, who was only too happy to have an additional paying student.

"During the year a young lady has been admitted to the School of Law," wrote Candler to the board the following June. Going on to refer to himself in the third person, he says, "The Chancellor did not oppose it, but he takes occasion to put on record that he does not approve the entrance of women into the Schools of Law, Medicine and Theology, believing that it is neither correct in principle nor wise in policy."

A year later, in the minutes of the meeting of June 7, 1919, Candler expounded on his view of the "folly" of coeducation:

> *At this session of the Board of Trustees the policy of the University with reference to co-education should be finally settled. In my judgment co-education is a mistaken policy. It is proper doubtless to open the Teachers College and the Summer Course for Teachers to female students, but in all other departments the University should be for male students only. The departments of medicine and law especially should not be open to women. Young men and young women working together in a dissecting room, or hearing together lectures on physiology and anatomy, would in my judgment create a most indelicate and injurious situation. And women lawyers would not promote justice in the courts.*
>
> *For one I cannot accept modern feminism in any of its lines of activity, and especially in the matter of higher education. God meant there should be two sexes in the world, and all the movements which seek to bring women into the sphere of men are what the great Horace Bushnell aptly called "reforms against nature." It would be just as reasonable to demand admittance for male students into the Wesleyan College at Macon, Ga., or to the Women's College at Lynchburg, Va., as to demand the admittance of female students to Emory University. The University should not compete with our Colleges for women. Moreover, our people are already educating nearly twice as many girls as boys, and there is no necessity for providing additional advantages in Emory University for female students. Young men need now more room than the institution has, or can provide at any time soon.*

The minutes of that 1919 meeting remain silent on whether the board even discussed the issue, but they apparently took no action against coeducation. In fact they did approve, at that meeting, the admission of girls to the preparatory academy started on the Oxford campus of Emory in 1915 as a wise use of that campus after Emory College moved to Atlanta. Otherwise, Candler's preferences seem to have been simply ignored; Eléonore Raoul received her law degree in 1920, and a "Miss C. B. Branham" received her MA from the graduate school that same year.

That year also brought two other significant changes: the ratification of the Nineteenth Amendment to the U.S. Constitution—giving women the right to vote—and the retirement of Bishop Candler as chancellor of Emory. Two years later the Candler faculty debated and then approved recommending the admission of women to the theology school. President Harvey Cox and the board of trustees quickly concurred in this recommendation.

Bishop Candler's animus against women's greater intellectual prospects comes through again in a reminiscence by Wyatt Aiken Smart, one of the first faculty members in the theology school. Writing in 1957, Smart recalled the bishop interrupting a discussion about the letter to the Hebrews, whose authorship was a subject of some dispute. One German scholar had theorized that the early female disciple Priscilla was the author. "The bishop said he knew that Priscilla did not write it, and for two reasons: first, that would put the feminist movement back into the Bible, and he didn't want it there; and secondly, it 'ain't got no postscript,' and no woman ever wrote a letter without a postscript."

Despite the 1922 decision by the Candler faculty to admit women, more than a decade passed before the first woman enrolled in the bachelor of divinity program. Most denominations at the time did not

*Mary Vaughn Johnson—"Mrs. Emmett Johnson" for the 1937* Campus *yearbook—was the first woman to earn the bachelor of divinity degree from Candler.*

ordain women, so women had little incentive to spend three years earning a degree required for an ordination that they could not have. Not until Mary Vaughn Johnson received her BD in 1938 did the barrier break. Johnson was the wife of Emmett S. Johnson, assistant professor of church administration and director of fieldwork. (She is listed in some records, such as Boone M. Bowen's list of graduates at the end of his history of Candler and even as author of her own BD dissertation, as "Mrs. Emmett S. Johnson.") Whether because she imagined her career to be that of a minister's wife, or because cultural limitations of the time channeled university women into domestic interests, the title of her thesis for the BD was "Job Analysis of a Mother of Preschool Children, as Indicated by Eight Mothers Whose Husbands Were Students in the Candler School of Theology Summer 1936." The thesis is a careful tolling of the hours devoted to cooking, childcare, housekeeping, and other chores that would keep, say, a parsonage in running order.

In the mid-1940s, women began enrolling in greater numbers for the master of religious education (later master of Christian education) degree; seven earned the degree in 1946, two more the next year, and after a gap of a year, nine more in 1949, and a continuing stream followed until the degree was discontinued in 1974 and replaced by the master of theological studies.

Only a few intrepid women followed Mary Johnson's lead to become bachelors of divinity. Twenty other women earned the BD through 1956, about half of them married

to Candler students. Several of these women went on to earn doctorates and teach religion. One, Sara Ann Wilkin 56T, was the first woman to preach at Glenn Memorial on the Emory campus. She served as a research associate for the International Greek New Testament Project, and in 1964, at the time of her appointment as instructor at Methodist College (now Methodist University), in Fayetteville, North Carolina, was finishing her PhD from Emory.

*Until the 1960s women who enrolled at Candler overwhelmingly pursued the master's degree in religious education.*

Although women were among the most devoted disciples of Jesus, and John Wesley licensed women to preach, official Methodism took a long time to authorize ordaining women. Only the Methodist Protestant Church did so before the twentieth century, and its merger with the Methodist Episcopal Church and the Methodist Episcopal Church, South (MECS), in 1939, set back women's ordination in Methodism for more than a decade, as the more conservative MECS weighed in and canceled the progress.

Other denominations had long been ordaining women: the Society of Friends since the early 1800s; the Congregationalist Church and Universalist Church since the mid-1800s; and even more conservative organizations like the Church of the

Nazarene, the Mennonites, the Church of God (Cleveland, Tennessee), and some Baptist denominations since the early twentieth century. But because the student body of Candler remained wholly Methodist until 1935, there was no pressure from outside Methodism and little pressure from inside Methodism to accommodate the calling of women to the ministry of Word and sacrament. Mission fields were fine, religious education okay, but preaching, baptizing, performing weddings, and celebrating the Eucharist—no.

Finally, the 1956 General Conference of the Methodist Church concluded that all paragraphs of the *Book of Discipline* pertaining to ordination and appointment should apply equally to women as well as to men. That same year, the Presbyterian Church (USA) authorized ordination of women. In another twenty years the Lutheran and Episcopal churches followed suit. The decision by mainline denominations to increase ministerial opportunities for women through ordination consequently increased the enrollment of women as students at Candler.

Change came slowly. In 1956 Sara Ann Wilkin was the sole woman in a BD class of 108, and the five women who earned master of Christian education degrees that year outnumbered the four men in the program. Over the next decade 16 more women earned BDs, more than half of them in 1965, compared to an average of 124 men each year.

Since the mid-sixties, the churches and the school have undergone a remarkable transformation. As more women sought ordination, especially in The United Methodist Church, the numbers of women at Candler began to reflect changes in the church. At the beginning of the 1970s, Dean James Laney reported that enrollment for the fall of 1970 included only 13 women—just 3 percent of the total of 421 students. Five years later that percentage had grown to 11, and in July 1978 Dean Waits reported that enrollment of women at Candler had grown to 17.6 percent of the total; in 1982 it was 24 percent. By the fall of 1986 fully 35 percent of entering students at Candler were women. This growing tide ebbed and flowed slightly, but it largely continued increasing until the first decade of the twenty-first century, when the enrollment of women at Candler reached a more or less steady level around 50 percent each year.

At the same time that women were knocking on the door to ordination and preparing to enter the MDiv program in far greater numbers, Candler was preparing to teach a noncredit program "designed to help women adjust" to the role of "minister's wife." This six-week course was initiated by Candler women in the early 1970s. Alvin Porteous, a visiting professor of theology, taught the class on contemporary theologians; Rod Hunter taught pastoral counseling; John Lawson taught "Basic Christian Beliefs"; and

Grant Shockley taught Christian education resources. Patti Wade, president of Candler Women at the time, noted, "Even though many of the wives are getting graduate degrees in their own fields, . . . we may not have this opportunity again to be near a higher education center that offers courses in the area we're involved in directly or indirectly as ministers' wives."

Roberta C. Bondi arrived at Candler in 1978 as the first woman appointed to a tenure-track position in the theology school.

## WOMEN ON THE FACULTY

The first women to have an affiliation with Candler in faculty or faculty-equivalent positions began appearing in Dean Laney's administration. As of 1970 the school had neither a female member of the regular faculty nor a single female affiliate or clinical instructor in the pastoral care track of the doctor of sacred theology (STD) degree, which Candler offered in collaboration with the Atlanta Interseminary Graduate Institute (now the Atlanta Theological Association). The next year Jane K. Kibler 66T became an affiliate member of the Georgia Mental Health Institute, which provided site supervision for STD students.

The faculty remained all male until Peggy Billings came to Candler as visiting professor of church and society in 1973. She was not entirely alone in the cohort of female "nonstudents" at the school. The administrative services were run by three women who might be thought of as the Candler answer to the Three Graces of classical mythology. These were "the three Helens"—Helen Banks, coordinator of supervised ministry; Helen Myler, the registrar; and Helen Stowers, the director of student aid and services.

In 1976 Adrienne Carr joined the faculty as an untenured lecturer in church education (she would later be promoted to assistant professor). Over the next two years women filled other temporary or nontenure positions: Elaine M. Amerson as assistant professor of Christian education; Nancy A. Hardesty as assistant professor of American church history; Phyllis Roe as coordinator of supervised ministry (replacing Helen Banks); and Nelia Kimbrough as assistant dean for student and academic services. All of these women served only briefly before leaving Candler.

Finally, more than half a century after the men on the Candler faculty voted to admit women to the school as students, another generation of Candler faculty men voted to admit women to their own club. The year was 1978, and the search for a new tenure-track assistant professor of patristics had led to a reluctant candidate who was teaching Semitic languages at the University of Notre Dame.

Roberta Chesnut had earned a BA from Southern Methodist University before heading off to Oxford University for her MA and DPhil degrees. Along the way she made a serendipitous choice. She decided that her interest in Semitic languages would be served best by a dissertation topic not in the Hebrew scriptures but in Syriac literature—an area of study that she thought had a small enough company of interested scholars that people would leave her in happy solitude as she pursued her research and writing. Syriac happened to be the language of much of the early church and, ultimately, her pathway

to the desert fathers and desert mothers, who in time became her own spiritual guides and the focus of much of her research.

Chesnut did not want to leave Notre Dame in 1978, however—especially for a Methodist seminary. Her own upbringing had left her with a sense of Methodism—indeed, Christianity and God—as oppressive and antiwoman, and it would take a lot of persuading to get her to Emory. Fortunately for Candler a committee of persuaders was close to her—those desert mothers and fathers, those *ammas* and *abbas*, who

Carol Ann Newsom, who arrived at Candler in 1980, was installed as Charles Howard Candler Professor of Old Testament in 2005.

appealed to her heart and mind to decide whether she would keep her relationship with them a kind of hobby or would finally begin to introduce them to a wider world through her teaching. She chose the second path, and it proved more difficult than even she imagined.

It is telling that the faculty minutes of the meeting when her appointment was announced, in October 1978, misspelled her last name as "Chestnut." In fact it took a while for her new faculty colleagues to get to know her. Having been due a sabbatical at Notre Dame, she negotiated leave at Candler for the fall and spring of 1978–79 and spent a lonely year largely absent from campus in an unfamiliar Atlanta as a single mother of two young children while preparing to teach to a predominantly male student body as a member of a wholly male faculty. By the time she resurfaced from her solitude and made her first plunge into the classroom, in the fall of 1979, she had remarried and become Roberta Bondi.

Almost immediately, Bondi was called upon to lead the search for a new faculty member. Frederick Prussner, professor of Old Testament, had died suddenly, and an expedited search for his successor was under way. Somehow the dean found it sensible to appoint as chair of the search committee the newest member of the faculty, with the least knowledge of the school, the university, the city, or the culture of a seminary, and so Bondi took up the task. Before long the short list of candidates for the Old Testament position had been narrowed to one, and in the spring of 1979 Carol Ann Newsom was offered the job of assistant professor. Meanwhile, she still had a dissertation to finish at Harvard University, and her official start was delayed until January 1, 1980—a day that would have been unlikely to find anyone in Bishops Hall to greet her.

Like Bondi, Newsom had given little or no thought to the possibility of teaching at a seminary. Educated in the liberal arts at Birmingham-Southern College (now University), she had set her course for a career in law by enrolling at Harvard Law School. (Curiously, a classmate at Harvard Law was a future dean of Candler, Kevin LaGree.) Realizing after a year and a half that the profession of law was not for her, Newsom entered Harvard Divinity School and earned an MTS before enrolling in the graduate school for her doctorate. Expecting to teach in a place like her old college, she found herself resisting the call from Candler but in the end accepted the invitation. More than thirty years later, she would look back on her career at Candler and declare that she would not trade seminary teaching for any other kind.

Such satisfactions lay far in the future, however. At Candler the job of the female faculty members entailed not only teaching, scholarship, and committee work but also enduring the effrontery of colleagues and students. One distinguished male colleague

*Rebecca Chopp, professor of systematic theology, became the first female provost at Emory in 1997.*

held forth in a faculty meeting—apparently in oblivious earnestness—about the problem of the growing number of women entering PhD programs, since these female scholars were likely to take jobs away from men, who after all were the breadwinners in their families. Both Bondi and Newsom were told that they had not been the first choice of some of their colleagues—just in case their self-confidence as pioneers in a wholly new terrain needed any more shaking. Bondi recalled, in retirement, that even into her third or fourth year of team teaching the introductory course in church history with William Mallard and Manfred Hoffmann, one male student regularly absented himself from the lectures on the days when she was scheduled to take the lectern.

Unfortunately support for these women faculty members beyond the confines of Candler was hard to find. Emory University was slow in appointing women to the faculty in general. Lore Metzger, an eminent scholar in comparative literature, arrived on campus in 1968 as the first woman appointed to the rank of full professor in Emory College. By 1975 the college had added only five more women to its faculty, and the few women on the faculties of the professional schools encountered oddities of behavior and decorum that have achieved the status of legend—except that they actually happened.

Time—and the appointment of more women at Candler—brought about a cultural shift. In the fifteen years (1978–93) following Bondi's appointment, nine more women arrived on the tenure track at Candler, and several others joined the ranks of nontenured faculty members and senior administrators. In 1991 the school launched a Program in Women's Studies with a part-time director, Kris Kvam; this program would be renamed the Program for Women in Theology and Ministry, and Belle Miller McMaster accepted appointment as the first full-time director in 1994.

Along the way, women moved increasingly into leadership positions. Nelia Kimbrough 74T began serving as assistant dean for student academic services even before she graduated, and she held that position for several years. Barbara Brown Taylor, a graduate of Emory College (class of 1973) and Yale Divinity School, served in a variety of administrative capacities in the late 1970s and early 1980s before setting off for her career as an Episcopal priest, author, and preacher. Jane Dammen McAuliffe, the first Candler faculty member internationally recognized for scholarship in Islamic studies, was appointed acting associate dean in 1991–92, and that same year Mary Lou Greenwood Boice was appointed to lead the admissions effort at Candler, the first woman in that position. (McAuliffe would leave for a deanship at Georgetown University and later the presidency of Bryn Mawr College.) Rebecca Chopp, who joined the faculty in 1987, was appointed dean of the faculty and academic affairs at Candler in July 1994 and served in that role until her appointment as the interim provost of Emory in July 1997—the most senior position ever held by a woman at the university to that point. (Chopp would leave Emory in 2001 to serve as dean of the Yale Divinity School for a year before assuming the presidencies of Colgate University and, later, Swarthmore College.)

With the appointment of Jan Love as dean of Candler in 2006, it appeared that the university had laid to rest, once and for all, Bishop Candler's sense that coeducation, let alone the place of women in theological education, was "folly." C

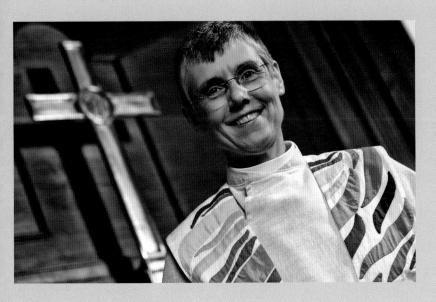

**HEATHER WARREN**  Heather Warren 82T was the first woman from Emory University to win a Rhodes scholarship and the second Rhodes scholar in Candler's history (the first was Edwin F. Moseley, in 1920). After her time at Oxford, Warren earned MA and PhD degrees from Johns Hopkins University. An ordained clergywoman, she teaches American religious history as a faculty member at the University of Virginia.

*The rear of Durham Chapel might have been more interesting than the front on this particular day.*

## CHAPTER SIX

# THE FORESIGHT OF "THE HOLY CLUB"

ALTHOUGH the late 1950s and 1960s brought dramatic improvements to Emory and to Candler—racial integration, strong leadership from President Sanford Atwood and others, excellent appointments to the faculties of the theology school and the university generally—the period also included some missed opportunities and losses.

At Candler, specifically, those losses came through the departure of faculty members whose later impact on the church and on scholarship would have redounded to the academic reputation of Candler. Instead, Candler became a line on their résumés as a way station on their progress toward eminence.

These faculty members included John B. Cobb Jr., an alumnus of Oxford College of Emory University, who left Emory and Candler for Claremont School of Theology in 1958. He established the school of process theology by integrating the philosophy of Alfred North Whitehead into Christian theology. James M. Robinson departed at the same time for the same place, where he would build a career as perhaps the best-known interpreter of Q and the Nag Hammadi library. (Both Cobb and Robinson left Emory in the company of Ernest Colwell, Candler alumnus and former president of the University of Chicago, whom President Goodrich White had recruited to Emory in 1953 as dean of the faculties with the prospect of Colwell's succeeding to the Emory presidency on White's retirement.

When the Emory board turned to S. Walter Martin instead, Colwell decamped for the presidency of Claremont.) Franklin Littell, a Methodist clergyman, theologian, and church historian regarded by many as one of the founders of Holocaust studies, left Candler for Southern Methodist University and later Temple University.

No doubt these defections from the Candler faculty were motivated in part by opportunities for different kinds of intellectual engagement elsewhere. They may have been prompted as well by the abysmally uncompetitive salaries that Candler paid in those days. (When Sanford Atwood became president of Emory in 1963, he set as one of his priorities the substantial enhancement of faculty salaries and soon launched a fund-raising campaign to accomplish that goal; despite his efforts, faculty salaries continued to lag through his presidency.) In any case, something about Candler appeared to be working well, but something else perhaps needed focused attention.

With the election of Dean Cannon to a bishop's office, the moment was right for a kind of decision about what sort of theology school Candler could or would become. Would it continue along the path it had set for itself in the previous half-century, as

*Hendrikus Boers (far left) leads a meeting of Common Program 400, an influential cross-disciplinary seminar for advanced graduate students and faculty in the Graduate Division of Religion. Also shown are Arthur Wainwright (second from left) and Max Miller (far right).*

a respectable, occasionally brilliant locus for the training of ministers to fill southern pulpits? Or would it attempt to continue doing that while adding something more? A solid enough foundation was in place for something more; the question was whether the university, the school, or anyone else had a vision for what could be built on top of it. A core of the Candler faculty thought they did have such a vision, and they were prepared to insist that the university come to share it.

According to the accounts of Boone Bowen and William Cannon, some behind-the-scenes competition to succeed Burton Trimble as dean of Candler in the early fifties had preceded the surprising, unannounced, and unsearched-for appointment of Cannon. The election of Cannon as bishop in 1968 precipitated the first time in the history of Candler that the dean would be chosen through a relatively open and representative search. By this time the university bylaws had been amended to spell out the consultative role of the faculty of each school in the appointment of its dean. "The Board of Trustees or its Executive Committee" was charged with approving the appointment "upon the recommendation by the president, who shall have conferred with an appropriate committee of the members of the faculty of the school."

Accordingly, with Cannon's departure, President Atwood appointed Mack Stokes as acting dean and formed a nine-member faculty search committee, chaired by then vice president and dean of the faculties Judson C. "Jake" Ward 33C 36G and comprising the heads of Candler's four curricular areas plus one additional faculty member from each area. (Ward was a longtime member of Glenn United Methodist Church, where he taught the "young adults" class for half a century until the youthfulness of many, including himself, had long passed; the class is now called the Jake Ward Class in his memory.) Atwood also appointed a four-member advisory committee chaired by Bishop Earl G. Hunt 46T (an Emory trustee and former president of Emory and Henry College, in Virginia). The advisory committee included D. W. Brooks, chair of the Committee of One Hundred, an Emory trustee, former CEO and chair of GoldKist, and, by his own account, advisor to every president from Franklin Roosevelt through Jimmy Carter. Brooks—for whom the commons area in Cannon Chapel is named—was one of a dwindling breed of prominent and very wealthy lay Methodists whose influence in church and educational matters matched their influence in national affairs.

With Mack Stokes in place as acting dean, some members of the faculty felt anxious about whether the outcome of the search was predetermined; they saw the inevitable removal of the word "acting" from his title. In the view of many, a

succession plan had been worked out. Certainly Stokes had considerable support among the faculty and the church: he had served Candler for seventeen years already, was held in esteem and affection by many, and had demonstrated administrative ability as director of the Graduate Division of Religion. Nevertheless, the search cast a wide net, as the committee considered more than fifty candidates and took its time to get the selection right.

Theodore Weber, professor of social ethics for more than a decade by this time, and a member of the search committee, would later recall that while visiting his in-laws in Connecticut in the winter of 1968–69, he dropped by the Yale Divinity School campus to catch up with friends and former colleagues. One person he visited was James Gustafson, the successor to H. Richard Niebuhr as the dean of Christian ethicists in the last quarter of the twentieth century. Gustafson had mentored a Yale alumnus and former missionary through the PhD program at Yale just a few years earlier, and that man, now nearing forty, had gone to Vanderbilt as assistant professor of Christian ethics and director of Methodist studies. Gustafson suggested to Weber that Candler should take a look at this man. Weber also spoke with Raymond Morris, who was the librarian at Yale Divinity School and a Methodist layman. Without knowledge of Weber's earlier conversation with Gustafson, Morris mentioned the same potential dean—James T. Laney.

Laney had been born in Arkansas and reared in Memphis and was the grandson (on his mother's side) of a learned and pious Methodist minister who shaped Laney's commitment to the church and his intellectual hunger. As covaledictorian of his 1945 graduating class at Central Memphis High School, Laney won a scholarship to Yale College, where he majored in economics. His undergraduate years had been interrupted by the draft and service in a U.S. Army counterintelligence unit in Korea, where he developed both affection for the country and its people and a sense of commitment toward helping the country overcome the debilitating effects of war. Returning to Yale, he graduated in 1950 and enrolled in divinity school, where he earned his bachelor of divinity in 1954 while serving as chaplain at Groton. After a stint as a Methodist pastor in Cincinnati, Ohio, he and his wife, Berta Radford Laney, set off for Korea in 1958 under the auspices of the Board of Missions of the Methodist Church. During the next five years, he became fluent in Korean, taught courses in theology and ethics at Yonsei University, and awakened to the call to spend his career in education.

To answer that call, the Laneys returned to the United States and Yale; by now they had five children, and with considerable urgency Jim Laney set out to finish his PhD in two years. After completing his dissertation on the theological ethics of Karl Barth,

Dietrich Bonhoeffer, and Paul Lehman, he packed up the family for Nashville, where he began teaching at the Vanderbilt Divinity School in 1966 while simultaneously serving Pegram Methodist Church outside the city.

The search committee at Candler soon set its sights on Laney and in time recommended him to President Atwood as the first choice to become the next dean of Candler. Even then his appointment was not a fait accompli. The faculty voted 13-8 for Laney, which prompted him to phone Weber and question the wisdom of accepting a deanship where more than a third of the faculty opposed his appointment. Weber sought to assure Laney that all would move to support him when he arrived.

Likewise, some bishops of the Southeastern Jurisdiction did not share the confidence in Laney's ability expressed by their colleague Bishop Hunt. According to William Mallard, a spate of telegrams arrived at President Atwood's office, including one from a bishop who said, "I am praying that you will not make a mistake"—in other words, praying that you will not hand the school to this new and unproven leader. Hearing of this from Laney (who had heard it from Atwood), Mallard, Weber, and a few others fired off a telegram to Laney: "We are praying that you will not make a mistake. Signed, the Holy Club." Probably appreciating the humorous reference to

*The theology faculty gathered on the steps of Bishops Hall in 1973.*

John and Charles Wesley's early Methodist organization at Christ Church, Oxford, as much as he appreciated the moral support, Laney did not make a mistake, and he arrived in the summer of 1969. Weber had predicted that those faculty members who had voted against Laney's appointment would soon come around, and this proved to be correct.

Apart from the first dean of the school—Plato Tracy Durham—Laney was the first appointed from beyond the Candler faculty. Among his strengths, as Boone Bowen notes in his history of Candler, Laney brought to Candler experience in the mission field (a significant focus of the school through its first decades), a clear commitment to and success in ministry to the local parish, superb academic preparation, sufficient administrative experience, and recent engagement with two of the leading seminaries in the country, Yale and Vanderbilt.

Dean Laney shifted into high gear the engine that Dean Cannon had ignited. Within four years Laney had increased the size of the Candler faculty by twelve positions—a growth of nearly 50 percent. At the same time, enrollment had risen 7.7 percent and tuition 25 percent, providing sufficient growth in income to offset the budgetary increase for personnel. (This pattern of increasing enrollment size

*Taking advantage of the hair styles of the day, Candler students in 1971 posed an interpretation of DaVinci's Last Supper, without the money bag of Judas as a prop.*

and tuition simultaneously to enlarge the budget would continue in Laney's Emory presidency, during which Emory College enrollment grew by almost 50 percent and tuition nearly doubled.)

Not only the number of faculty increased; the quality of Laney's appointments began to lift the scholarly reputation of the school in short order. Justo Gonzalez, the prolific and influential Cuban-born Methodist theologian and church historian, had been appointed by Cannon but began his eight years at Candler during Laney's first semester as dean, introducing to Candler the development of Latino theology. Laney's own first appointment was Harry Moon, assistant professor of sacred music, who launched programs like the Choraliers, which became a central aspect of the Candler community life over the next forty years.

Among Laney's other early appointments were several whose impact would resonate throughout the university, the church, and the academy generally:

- Grant Shockley, professor of Christian education and the first African American to serve full-time on Candler's faculty. He went on to serve as president of the Interdenominational Theological Center and, later, Philander Smith College, while becoming one of the eminent contributors to Christian education in the black church in the twentieth century.
- E. Brooks Holifield, later Charles Howard Candler Professor of Church History and in 2001, the year of his retirement from Candler, an inductee into the prestigious American Academy of Arts and Sciences—the first clergy member of the Emory faculty to be elected to the AAAS since Atticus Haygood in 1883.
- Charles V. Gerkin, former chaplain of Grady Memorial Hospital in Atlanta and founding executive secretary of the Georgia Association for Pastoral Care (now the Care and Counseling Center of Georgia), who became one of the giants in the field of clinical pastoral education.
- Leander E. Keck, who as professor of New Testament also chaired the Graduate Division of Religion for seven years before leaving to become dean of Yale Divinity School.
- Donald W. Shriver Jr., who served as professor of ethics and society and director of the DMin program before he was named president of Union Theological Seminary in New York in 1975.

Laney also brought to Candler the first woman to teach on the faculty. Peggy Billings, who was then an assistant general secretary of the Women's Division of the Board of Global Missions of The United Methodist Church, taught religion and

**MACK STOKES** Though he was not a Candler alumnus (he had degrees from Asbury College, Duke Divinity School, and Boston University), Mack B. Stokes came to be identified closely with the theology school he helped to shape and the doctoral program in religion he helped to launch. Joining the Candler faculty in 1943, he was the first chaired professor at Candler, appointed to the brand-new Franklin Parker Chair in Systematic Theology when it was created in 1953. He also served as the first associate dean of Candler, appointed by Dean Cannon to help build up the newly formed Graduate Division of Religion when the Emory trustees approved the PhD track in religion in 1958. After thirty-one years of teaching thousands of preachers and "theologs," Stokes was elected as a bishop of The United Methodist Church in 1972, four years after the creation of that new denomination. Assigned to the Jackson, Mississippi, area, he played a key role in the merging of four segregated conferences (two African American and two white) into two integrated conferences, which were the forerunners of the current Mississippi Conference.

"He served in Mississippi at an important time," said retired bishop Kenneth Lee Carder, who was the Jackson area bishop from 2004 to 2008. "He brought to that task not only a pastoral sensitivity but also a deep theological grounding for reconciliation."

Similar sensitivity and grounding had served Stokes during his acting deanship between the administrations of his good friend Bill Cannon and his successor, Jim Laney, who came to credit Stokes for consummate graciousness and professional commitment in smoothing the transition to Laney's leadership. Stokes also built many bridges between the school and the church. As a bishop, he served Emory as a trustee and continued to attend board meetings long after being elevated to emeritus status in 1980. In 2008 he and his wife, Rose, established the Bishop Mack B. and Rose Y. Stokes Chair in Theology at Candler.

Mack Stokes died on November 21, 2012, one month to the day shy of his 101st birthday.

society for the year 1972–73, and her impact was such that the faculty began a search to fill a full-time appointment with a female scholar.

By 1975 the building efforts of Cannon and Laney had lifted the national profile of the Candler School of Theology and secured its reputation among the top theological institutions in America. That year, *Change* magazine, in a ranking of professional schools in North America, recognized Candler as the sixth-best theology school, behind only the divinity schools of Harvard, Yale, and Chicago, and the theological seminaries at Princeton and Union in New York.

Much of the credit for that rise in reputation rests with the faculty members who were publishing books and articles, preaching and teaching in churches throughout the Southeast, and mentoring students who graduated into pulpits around the country or went on to their own places in the professoriate. The school had experienced firsthand many of the tremendous dislocations that had transformed American society since the end of World War II. Indeed, the theology faculty had laid the groundwork for some of those transformations in Atlanta and at Emory—and the faculty had risen to meet those challenges by creatively adapting their role in the formation of ministers. Without abdicating their commitment to scholarship of the highest order, the faculty had proposed, considered, and undertaken innovative ways to prepare ministers of the church to serve in a society undergoing rapid change.

From 1953, when about 50 percent of American homes owned television sets, to 1975, when nearly every home did, the Candler faculty added media training to its tool kit and took on an integral role in the development of the Protestant Radio and Television Center on Clifton Road (see chapter 3). From 1961, when Candler enrolled no African American students, to 1977, when Candler instituted an affirmative action plan and enrolled a student body that was about 6 percent African American, the Candler faculty added three African Americans to its number and developed collaborations with the historically black institutions at the Interdenominational Theological Center. In a period when social strictures of all kinds were being broken, when the voting age was lowered, and when the youth of America were demanding a place at every table, the Candler faculty began engaging students by giving them a voice in decision making, requiring their active collaboration in contextual education, and nurturing the formation of mature Christians as well as seasoned scholars. As some of these faculty members would later recall, much of the hard work in preparing for the growth of the 1970s had been done by that core of faculty that Dean Cannon had appointed in the mid- to late 1950s.

Still, the energy, vision, and gracious panache that Dean Laney brought to the school certainly drove it forward and upward. By the fall of 1976, in his last year as dean, enrollment had climbed to 588 from 427 during his eight-year deanship—a growth of 37 percent that made Candler the largest United Methodist seminary in the world at the time. This growth mirrored the expansion of the Emory University student body during Sanford Atwood's presidency, but it stands out among theology schools nationwide during the period.

Laney had guided the faculty in instituting new measures for reviewing promotion and tenure, ushering in a degree of shared governance, consultation, and accountability in faculty appointments that simply had not existed prior to his arrival. In leading this faculty, Laney helped lift the profile of the school to national prominence in several ways.

First, he guided the faculty in reshaping the congeries of field placements he inherited, as Candler created an innovative program of supervised ministry. Key to this effort was the appointment of Charles "Chuck" Gerkin, who had served as the first chaplain of the large and historic Grady Memorial Hospital in Atlanta during the tense time of its integration. Having ministered in the parish as well as in

*The eminent Cuban-born theologian Justo Gonzalez (in suit and tie) taught at Candler from 1969 to 1977.*

clinical settings (he would serve as president of the Association for Clinical Pastoral Education in the 1970s), Gerkin had a keen understanding of the importance of making neophyte ministers familiar with sometimes discomfiting situations.

By the 1971–72 academic year, the faculty had devised a three-year program of supervised ministry as an integral part of the curriculum. The program—later dubbed contextual education, or "ConEd"—was the first of its kind in the country. Most theological schools at the time required some level of supervised fieldwork. The Supervised Ministry Program at Candler, however, required the new ingredient of full collaboration of the faculty with field supervisors to foster, in small groups of students, the kind of theological reflection about the field experience that would enlarge their understanding of ministry. The concept did not always translate easily into practice. Some faculty members, trained as academics in fields less directly related to ministry, did not always feel competent or comfortable in guiding theological discussions about the Veterans Administration hospital or a homeless shelter. The emphasis in the early years on the model of clinical pastoral education loaded conversations heavily with psychological language and sometimes pushed students and faculty alike to withdraw or rebel. The program has undergone several alterations in the decades since it was incorporated, but it continues to stand out as a national model for the training of clergy.

Laney's second means of lifting the national profile of Candler was in listening to his librarian, Channing Jeschke, as the two of them seized on the opportunity to create a world-class research library at Emory. Following a hunch and a nose for acquisitions, Jeschke persuaded his dean in 1975 to purchase the Hartford Theological Seminary library collection, which had just gone on the market. This collection would enrich the depth of materials at Candler and Emory to support research programs in religion. Laney undertook the hard sell to the Emory board of trustees for approval of the $1.25 million offer from Candler, and he then returned to meet with the board a second time when the asking price ballooned to $1.75 million to counter the offer of $2 million from the Billy Graham Association. After the deal was concluded, every library journal, every theology periodical, and most major newspapers in the country reported the historic transfer, giving Candler a level of publicity and academic cachet it had never experienced. (See chapter 7 for a full account of this acquisition.)

A third contribution Laney made to the future of Candler often goes unremarked upon and uncelebrated. In the fall of 1974, after five years in office, Laney took a sabbatical leave and spent the term at Harvard Divinity School as a visiting professor. While he was there, intimations came his way that the deanship at Harvard might

Don Saliers (left) holds one of the Eucharistic elements during the last worship service in Durham Chapel, in 1976.

open up for him if he were interested. Returning to Atlanta in mid-autumn for the annual meeting of the Emory board of trustees, Laney prudently shared word of this dance invitation (it was hardly a firm proposal) with the board chairman, Henry Bowden, who suggested that he wait and consider what might develop when President Atwood stepped down. Atwood announced the following spring that he would retire in two years. Thus began Laney's storied path to and through the Emory presidency.

But that sabbatical semester gave Laney an opportunity to size up both the competition and the future. The faculty at Harvard, while fulfilling a mission different from those of the faculty at Candler and Yale, certainly ranked among the top half-dozen divinity faculties in the country, so viewing it up close gave Laney a sense of the advantages and liabilities at Candler. More significantly, that autumn in Cambridge introduced him to a passel of young scholars who were either junior faculty at Harvard or doctoral students about to wrap up their dissertations and advance into the professoriate. These included James W. Fowler (Harvard PhD, 1971), who arrived at Candler in 1978 and would make Candler internationally synonymous with his transformative theories of faith development and his work directing the Center for Research in Faith and Moral Development; Carol A. Newsom (Harvard MTS, 1975; PhD, 1982), who arrived at Candler in 1980 and would achieve international recognition for her Dead Sea Scrolls translations and commentaries, as well as her coeditorship of *The Women's Bible Commentary* and the *New Oxford Annotated Bible*; David S. Pacini (Harvard MTS, 1972; MA, 1974; PhD, 1979), who arrived in 1980 and almost immediately undertook the codirectorship of one of the first major international symposia at Emory; and Steven M. Tipton (Harvard PhD, 1979), who joined the Candler faculty in 1979 and would soon contribute to one of the more influential critiques of individualism in American life, *Habits of the Heart*. Frank Alexander, who was completing MTS and JD degrees at Harvard during that period, had extensive conversations with Laney at the time and was later recruited to Emory Law School, where he helped found the Center for the Study of Law and Religion.

In a sense, Laney scouted the competition (or the competition's farm team) and provided the reports that his successor, Jim Waits, would use to recruit a whole new roster of players.

One other scholar who may have surfaced during Laney's sojourn in New England and would come to the faculty during Waits's deanship was Jon P. Gunnemann, an assistant professor at Yale and, like Laney, a Yale PhD graduate who had written his dissertation under James Gustafson's direction. Laney also had occasion in the fall of 1974 to journey to the University of Chicago Divinity School, where he renewed his friendship with Gustafson, who had left Yale for Chicago some years before. In 1988 Laney would lure Gustafson to Emory as the Henry R. Luce Professor in Humanities and Comparative Studies, and Gustafson would remain on the Emory faculty for ten years before retiring in 1998 as the Robert W. Woodruff Professor of Comparative Studies and Religion.

When, in the spring of 1977, the Emory board of trustees announced that Jim Laney would become the seventeenth president of Emory, the Candler School of Theology was well positioned to carry on the successful development encouraged by that "Holy Club" when it fired off its telegram to Nashville in 1969. For along with all the other initiatives and appointments Laney had made during his eight years as dean, he had brought to Candler an outstanding lieutenant, one who would continue the remarkable advancements over the next fourteen years. *C*

*Robert W. Woodruff, right, confers a congratulatory blessing on James T. Laney, who had just been inaugurated as president of Emory. Laney served as president from 1977 to 1993 after leading the Candler school as dean from 1969 to 1977.*

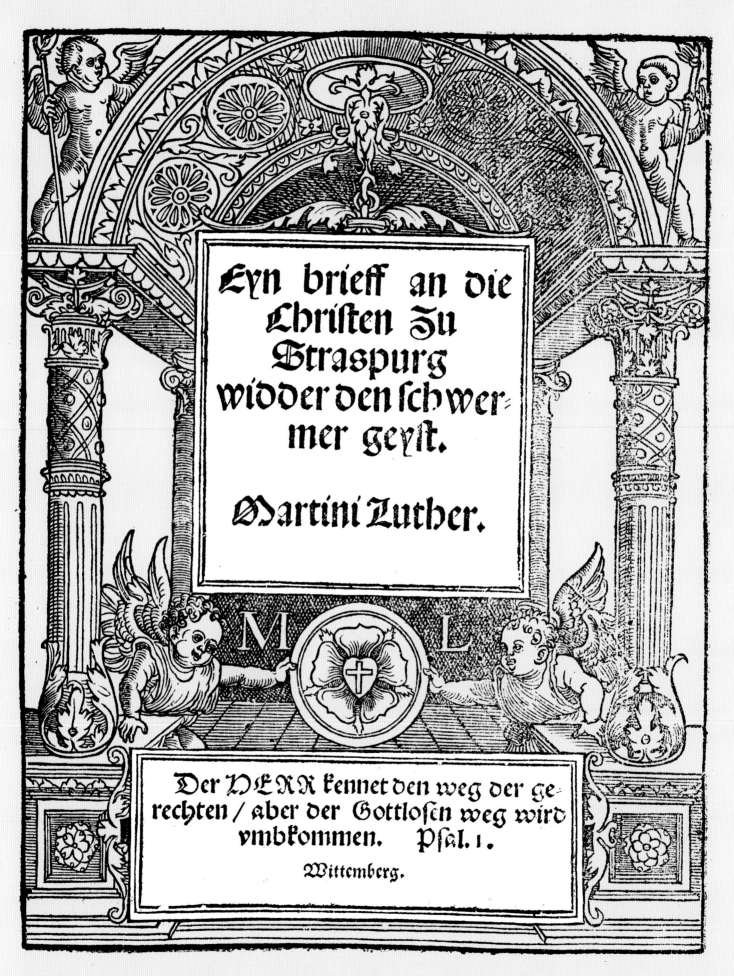

Eyn brieff an die Christen zu Straspurg widder den schwermer geyst.

Martini Luther.

Der HERR kennet den weg der gerechten / aber der Gottlosen weg wird vmbkommen. Psal. 1.

Wittemberg.

The "Luther Rose" appears on the title page of Martin Luther's 1524 work Eyn brieff an die Christen zu Strasburg widder den schwermer geyst. The rose serves as the logo for the Digital Image Archive of the Pitts Theology Library.

## CHAPTER SEVEN

# A Brilliant Jewel: The Pitts Theology Library

WHEN the Candler School of Theology took up quarters in Wesley Memorial Church in 1914, the faculty and students had at their disposal one of the more remarkable church libraries in the Southeast at the time, with a trove of rare books and manuscripts from the first generation of Methodists.

These materials may have had great intrinsic value and high potential for future scholars, but it is unclear whether they had any direct usefulness to the curriculum for teaching novice pastors how to minister to the church in a new century. The bulk of the library had come to Wesley Memorial through the palavering skills of Bishop Warren Candler.

Just three years previously, Candler had learned that a collection of Wesleyana, gathered by an Englishman named F. Thursfield Smith, was being offered for sale, and the bishop hoped to bring these treasures to Atlanta. By hard negotiation with the late Mr. Smith's son, Candler acquired the whole collection for $5,000 ($2,290 below its appraised value), and Wesley Memorial became home to some twenty-five hundred rare books as well as manuscripts and letters of the Wesleys, Bishop Thomas Coke, and other Methodist notables. Within weeks of the opening of the school in September 1914, Bishop Candler had the opportunity to add to

the Wesleyana collection through the granddaughter of Bishop John Christian Keener, who had died after amassing a number of Methodist treasures. Whatever insight this gathering of materials from the founders of Methodism offered to the scholarship of modernist high critics or biblical literalists, the collection did include Bishop Francis Asbury's razor, his New Testament, and a wax life mask of John Wesley purported to be "the only original likeness of Wesley in America."

While students in the new school of theology who saw these curiosities in 1914 may have gained inspiration and strength in their Methodist calling, no evidence exists that these museum pieces added much to the intellectual development of future theologians or the practical development of budding pulpiteers. Still, by 1939 other purchases and gifts of Wesley material had made the Wesleyana collection at Candler one of the best in the world at the time, second only to the combined collections of Wesley's City Road Chapel and the Methodist Publishing House in London.

A long time would pass, however, before the theology library—or any other library at Emory, for that matter—achieved eminence. In 1915 the university trustees authorized a budget of two thousand dollars for books and periodicals in the theology library, and all of this sum was needed simply to begin catching up to the kind of collections

*The theology library in the 1930s offered Spartan surroundings for study.*

already in place at Vanderbilt and Duke, not to mention the long-established libraries at divinity schools like Harvard and Yale. By the time the school moved to the Druid Hills campus in Atlanta in the summer of 1916, the library assets amounted to no more than ten thousand dollars.

During its early years the library added only about 200 volumes a year, and in the lean years of the Great Depression the annual book budget fell to a mere five hundred dollars. In 1937 Dean Franklin N. Parker noted the relative poverty of the theology library compared to the collections of competing seminaries. While the library of the theology school held just under 14,000 volumes in 1937, the Drew Theological School owned 169,000; Garrett Theological Seminary, 189,089; Princeton Theological Seminary, 146,309; Southern Baptist Seminary in Louisville, Kentucky, 40,000; and the Union Theological Seminary in Richmond, 50,000. More serious study of theology could be done elsewhere, and Dean Parker considered the addition of books, the acquisition of more Methodist research materials, and subscriptions to religious and theological periodicals to be "the greatest need of our School at the present time."

As a result of impoverished development during the first decades at Candler, when the end of World War II brought a boom to theological education in America the theology library held fewer than 39,000 volumes to support ministerial programs. This number would have to increase dramatically as the university administration contemplated the advent of a doctoral program in religion.

In October 1945 the Emory trustees approved the proposal by the administration to move into the ranks of research universities and begin offering the PhD. The doctorate in religion was still more than a decade away; the first PhD programs at Emory were chemistry and biochemistry, with anatomy, biology, English, and history added in 1949, and psychology in 1951. Providing adequate support for scholarly research in theology and religion meant hiring additional faculty and acquiring a much more substantive collection of materials than either the theology library or the university library then held (the Robert W. Woodruff Library would not be dedicated until 1969, and meanwhile the Asa G. Candler Library–Candler Library, as distinct from "Candler's library"–served as the main library of the university).

Not until 1958, with the theology collection approaching 60,000 volumes and the addition of first-rate scholars to the faculty, did the graduate school approve the doctorate in biblical studies. In just five years the theology collections had grown by 30 percent, and the budget for books and periodicals had doubled. In her 1959 report to the dean, Elizabeth Royer, the librarian, noted joyfully, "This has been the finest year in the history of the library." Exclamation marks were not included but might

Using the office that once served as the university chancellor's office, Channing Jeschke oversaw the development of a major research collection at Pitts Library.

have been. More significantly, the library had expanded its purpose from its original mission. Now, in addition to "preserving the church's story" in order "to enhance the church's ministry," the library was intended to support preparation of both the next generation of ministers and the professoriate that would teach them.

The growth of the theology library in its first sixty years required the gradual annexation of the entire building in which it was planted. The first academic building constructed in Druid Hills (along with its twin, the old law school, later the Sociology Building and now Michael C. Carlos Hall), the Theology Building originally housed the chancellor's office, faculty offices, classrooms, and the university chapel in addition to the library. Occupying only the west wing of the first floor of the building, the library lacked fans and window shades or draperies, and thus exposed books and students alike to sun, heat, and probably insects. In 1937, the growing collection and a larger student body required expanding the library space, so a part of the basement was converted into a room for book stacks. Nineteen years later, the addition of research materials to support the PhD programs led to renovation of the rest of the basement for stacks.

The most dramatic alteration of the building came in 1975–76, when the purchase of the Hartford Theological Seminary collection presented Emory with the choice of either building a new theology library three times the size of the old one, or turning the entire theology edifice over to the library and erecting another structure to house the displaced chapel, offices, and classrooms. With time short and books needing to be moved from Hartford, Connecticut, to Atlanta, the university opted for the quick solution and made the whole building a library. Emory commissioned the internationally renowned architect Paul Rudolph to design a renovation of the Theology Building, and on November 11, 1976, the building was officially rededicated for use solely as the Pitts Theology Library.

The story of this transformation began with Elizabeth Royer's retirement from the theology librarianship. As she prepared to step down in 1971 after thirty-nine years with Candler—thirty-eight of them as director of the library—the search for her successor led to a well-prepared Yankee minister and librarian named Channing R.

Jeschke. Educated at Oberlin College, he earned an MDiv from Yale Divinity School before completing his PhD in church history at the University of Chicago and then picking up a library degree from the best library school in the country, at Columbia University. Along the way he sharpened his antiquarian instincts as assistant rare book librarian at Union Theological Seminary in New York, then served as librarian and assistant professor of theological bibliography at Berkeley Divinity School, the Episcopal seminary associated with Yale. He was serving there when he was invited to interview for the Candler job in 1971.

The Candler dean at the time, James Laney, had known Jeschke at Yale Divinity School, and the conversation during Jeschke's interview inevitably turned to comparisons between Candler and Yale. Years later Jeschke would recall asking Laney what kind of library he wanted Candler to have. When Laney replied, "A library like the one at Yale," Jeschke promised that with the right support, he could give it to Laney in a year. Jeschke was given the job, and as it turned out, he was not far off in his prediction.

*The "Wesley Pulpit," an artifact in Pitts Theology Library, was built by Welsh miners for John Wesley to use at an outdoor gathering.*

Louis Pasteur famously said that "chance favors the prepared mind." Jeschke's mind was certainly prepared, and a year after he arrived at Candler, chance came his way in an announcement that had nothing to do with libraries. In 1972 the trustees of the Hartford Theological Seminary voted to change the mission of the school. With four of the nation's top theology schools—Harvard, Yale, Union, and Princeton—less than three hours' drive from Hartford, the competition for MDiv students had grown excessively daunting; Hartford therefore decided to change its focus. No longer would it prepare men and women for ordination to the clergy; it would offer continuing education, conduct research into congregational life, and study the church in society and the world.

Hartford traced its founding to 1833, however, and had accumulated a library on a par with the best. Its former librarian, Ernest Cushing Richardson, had spent at least a decade traveling Europe with a healthy stipend at his disposal to gather books that he thought

*Wesleyana from the Thursfield Smith Collection—including Francis Asbury's razor, shown here—graced the library at Wesley Memorial in Atlanta when the Candler school held its first classes there in 1914.*

necessary for research. (Richardson developed his own cataloguing system, later called the "Princeton System" because of his subsequent decades of service as director of the Princeton University library, where he applied it.) In 1972 the Hartford library owned one of the most extensive collections of Reformation materials in North America, especially writings by Martin Luther, as well as an unsurpassed collection of hymnody, and materials from the church in Asia and Africa.

When Jeschke read of the change of focus at Hartford, he realized that most of its library collection would be of little use to that seminary in view of its new curricula. As another Emory writer has quoted him as saying, "It dawned on me that what had been their jewel would become their white elephant."

To help relieve the Hartford trustees and administration of their white elephant, Laney and Jeschke spent three years negotiating the purchase of the Hartford collection for Emory. During part of that time, in the fall of 1974, Laney was on sabbatical at Harvard Divinity School, where he helped fend off the possible depredations of SUNY Stony Brook on the Hartford collection. The prospect was touch and go, as other prospective buyers offered bids. Among them was the Billy Graham organization, which wanted the collection for the Billy Graham Center Library at Wheaton College in Illinois and offered more than Emory could muster.

In the end, with foundation support and private donations, the university was able to max out its bid at $1.75 million for the 220,000 volumes up for sale—an average of eight dollars a book for a collection that included polyglot editions of the Bible dating back centuries and unique treasures like a copy of Luther's 1528 Psalter owned by reformer Ambrosius Blaurer and filled with his corrections, annotations, and whimsical drawings. With the stroke of a pen on a purchase contract, the Candler School of Theology had added decades of acquisition to the storehouse of knowledge in its library. Without time for the slow accretion of materials, Jeschke had needed to buy in bulk, and he had succeeded in acquiring in short order the kind of theology library that more established seminaries had needed decades, if not centuries, to build.

When the Emory trustees approved the purchase, and Hartford signed off on the deal, Jeschke immediately began organizing one of the largest transfers of books in American history. Later correspondence would reveal disagreement between officials at Hartford and those at Emory about a few specifics of the transaction. The announcement by Sotheby Parke Bernet Inc. offering the Hartford collection for sale indicated that it was "understood to comprise over two hundred thousand volumes." Three components—an Islamic collection of some 30,000 volumes, a 10,000-volume collection serving the Church and Ministry Program at Hartford, and a smaller collection from the estate of a donor—were excluded from the sale, along with certain manuscripts. The Hartford librarian put the size of the entire library at around 256,000, minus the 40,000 for the exempted portions, which left just under 220,000 volumes up for sale. Negotiations between the two schools apparently used the figure "200,000" repeatedly. The *New York Times* reported the sale on August 21, 1976, as "the 900-mile transfer of 240,000 books," along with some 8,700 linear feet of pamphlets and periodicals. The shipping manifests for the two moving companies used to transport the books note that one company moved 1,794 cartons, each containing an average of 24 books, while the other moved 7,545 cartons of books, periodicals, and pamphlets. However it was tabulated, it was a lot of books. (Jeschke always stuck with the figure of 220,000.) As Jeschke would remark for years to come, "Never before in the history of American higher education has a book collection of this size and quality been transferred from one institution to another over so many miles."

What made the purchase most stunning was the degree to which the two collections complemented each other. Raymond Morris, the librarian emeritus of the Yale Divinity School, who served as a consultant and appraiser of the Hartford collection for Emory, reported that Hartford had acquired most of its material before the Candler School of Theology was even founded. He noted that in 1930, when the library at Candler had just over 8,000 volumes and an acquisitions budget of $678, the Hartford library held 188,000 volumes, spent nearly five times as much on acquisitions, and added nearly as many books every year as Candler owned at the time.

Overnight, the arrival of the Hartford collection pushed the holdings of the Pitts Theology Library from around 90,000 volumes in 1972 to more than 300,000. The library jumped from forty-fifth-largest theological library in North America to sixth or seventh (eventually Pitts would rise to second, before falling behind Union and Princeton seminaries). The total cost of purchasing and moving the Hartford

*Margaret Pitts (left) was for decades the great patron of the theology library. She is shown here in 1973 with Dean James Laney and Mattie Trimble, widow of Dean Burton Trimble.*

**MARGARET PITTS** Around her hometown of Waverly Hall, Georgia, some eighty-eight miles southwest of Atlanta and just down the road from FDR's Little White House in Warm Springs, she was always Miss Margaret. At Emory she was Miss Pitts.

When Margaret Adger Pitts died in July 1998 at the age of 104, her legacy at the Candler School of Theology had long been established, and yet still greater legacy would come. Her estate was valued at $192 million, nearly half of which was bequeathed to Candler, while the rest was apportioned to several other United Methodist interests in South Georgia.

William Irby Hudson Pitts, Miss Margaret's father, enjoyed a similarly long life—1862 to 1964. Between those years he flourished in his native Waverly Hall and left only for a short stint of business school in Atlanta and a year's employment in Columbus, Georgia. Taking over his father's mercantile business, Pitts built up the general store, invested wisely in Coca-Cola, and developed a number of other business interests into a multimillion-dollar enterprise. Along the way he practiced generous philanthropy to Methodist causes and fostered similar habits in the youngest of his three children, Margaret.

Never marrying, Miss Pitts devoted herself to the Methodist Church and to its educational institutions. LaGrange College and Andrew College, not far from her home in opposite directions, both benefited from her largesse, as did the South Georgia Methodist Home for Children, Epworth-by-the-Sea on St. Simons Island, and churches around Waverly Hall. As a lifetime trustee of the William I. H. and Lula E. Pitts Foundation, established by her father in 1941, Miss Pitts guided the foundation in helping to underwrite the purchase of the Hartford collection, and in 1976 the renovated building was named the Pitts Theology Library to honor her father and her.

At the dedication of the library on November 11, 1976, Channing Jeschke—later named the Margaret A. Pitts Professor of Theological Bibliography—paid tribute to the staunchest supporter of the library. He commented on her "belief in the importance of excellence in the preparation of persons for the ministry and her generous support of this library that bears her family name." Such generosity, he said, was "a singular witness to her faith and a testimony for all of us." Proclaiming that "Miss Pitts represents Georgia at its finest," he addressed her personally: "Miss Pitts, you are Candler School of Theology's candidate for Miss Georgia of 1976 or any other year."

collection, as well as renovating and expanding the building to house the new Pitts Theology Library, amounted to $3,450,000.

Significantly, the holdings of the Hartford collection helped shape the decisions about what Pitts Library should emphasize in its future acquisitions. For any library, the limits of space and budget mean hard choices about what to collect, and despite its recent windfall, Pitts Library had limitations. Knowing both the strengths of the bulked-up Pitts Library as well as the interests of the Candler faculty, and counting into the mix the important subjects in which other theology libraries either were or were not collecting, Jeschke decided to build special collections in four areas: materials related to the Reformation in Germany, English religious materials from 1660 until World War I, theological dissertations of the seventeenth and eighteenth centuries, and primary and periodical literature of the African churches.

The first of these areas was well represented in the Hartford books, with many first editions of Luther's works as well as those of his lieutenant Philipp Melanchthon, his confessor Staupitz, and his teacher Karlstadt, and dozens of works by opponents of Luther, like Erasmus, Cochlaeus, and Eck. In October 1987 Richard C. Kessler, a Lutheran layman who had begun to collect rare imprints and manuscripts of Luther, donated his collection and signed an agreement to support development of the Richard C. Kessler Reformation Collection, which by 2013 had grown to contain more than thirty-five hundred pieces written by Luther and his colleagues or opponents and published before 1570. The Kessler Collection ranks among the most impressive resources for Reformation studies in the United States and has no parallels in the South. Guided by a steering committee chaired by Kessler and including the theology dean and librarian, the ongoing development of the collection also provides occasion every year to celebrate Reformation Day through exhibitions, lectures, and musical performances.

By the vagaries of history, the second major area of development in Pitts Library—English religious history since 1660 and the restoration of the monarchy—is intertwined with the first. The English Reformation took many of its cues from Luther, and John Wesley's own transforming experience of regeneration occurred during his reading of Luther's commentary on Paul's Epistle to the Romans. Materials acquired in this area since 1972 number in the tens of thousands and hold value not only for their use in research but also for their unique place in church history. Prominent in this area is the personal library of Cardinal Henry Edward Manning (1808–92), a major influence in the First Vatican Council and, along with Cardinal John Henry Newman, one of the leading English Catholics of the nineteenth century.

Complementing the Manning collection, the library in 1984 purchased some seven thousand books and sixteen manuscript collections relating to English Roman Catholic history and theology. Gathered by James Molloy, a scholar and churchman from Milton, England, these materials include books by and on Sir Thomas More, including first editions of his work as well as books printed secretly in England during the Elizabethan era. Alongside the Molloy and Manning collections, the Pitts holdings in Wesleyana, nonconformist materials, and Anglican materials provide a picture window on the panorama of English religious life.

The third area of special collections comprises theological disputations and dissertations published in northern Europe during the seventeenth and eighteenth centuries, a period that formed an important bridge between the Reformation and the ongoing development of Protestantism in the nineteenth century. The fourth area gathers materials from the fast-growing body of Christianity in Sub-Saharan Africa. Much of this material is archival or consists of periodicals—printed pieces that are of the moment, evanescent, easily overlooked or discarded, but possibly vital to future historians who will write the history of Christianity on that continent.

Curiously, one of the great strengths of the Hartford collection that did not provide a focus for Jeschke's collecting was the Warrington-Pratt-Soule Collection of Hymnody and Psalmody. Developed by three different collectors, this extraordinary repository included rare books of hymns and psalms dating from Calvin's Geneva, through early-American shape-note hymnals, to the denominational hymnals of the late nineteenth century. During the first decades of the twenty-first century, the hymnody collection at Pitts has been augmented significantly and is perhaps second in size only to that of the Library of Congress. With funding from the National Endowment for the Humanities, Pitts Library has preserved thousands of these brittle volumes on microfilm. An important addition of Sacred Harp tune books (first published in Bremen, Georgia, and since spread across the country) has provided the occasion for the annual Emory Sacred Harp Sing in Cannon Chapel. Of significant interest to Methodist hymn enthusiasts, the notebooks of the great hymn writer Fred Pratt Green have joined other archival materials at Pitts Library. Green, a British Methodist minister as well as poet and hymnist, received an honorary doctorate from Emory in June 1982, during the convocation of the Hymn Society of America on Emory's campus.

By the time Channing Jeschke retired in 1994, after twenty-three years at Candler, he had transformed the rather unexceptional library he had found when he arrived. The collection was almost peerless, and he had addressed other matters almost as arduously as he had filled the shelves. He fought a constant and not always successful battle to keep the needs of the library foremost on the growing list of competing priorities of the theology school. A decade after the Hartford acquisition, for instance, Jeschke noted in his 1986 annual report that Pitts had experienced "gradual movement toward achieving parity with the older, established theological libraries," but its staff salaries and staff size both remained the lowest among the top six theological libraries (Union, Harvard, Princeton, Graduate Theological Union, and Southwest Baptist were the others).

Five years later, in 1991, besetting budgetary issues loomed. During the 1980s, he reported, the collections at Pitts grew faster every year than did those of any of its peers, but the budget for operations fell grievously behind. Having started the decade $130,000 below the average operations budget for the other top five libraries, Pitts ended the decade $236,000 below. The library was losing ground in its ability to process acquisitions, update information technology, and preserve the rare materials that were prey to time (among these materials were thousands of books printed on highly acidic paper in the nineteenth and early twentieth centuries that needed to be microfilmed).

Jeschke dreamed of raising funds to build a Tuscan-style, campanile-like structure between the theology library and Cannon Chapel to house the rare books and archives. In reality, it was difficult enough to persuade the university to find funds for replacing the rotted roof underlayment, waterproofing the leaky foundation, upgrading the air-handling systems, and installing proper fire safeguards.

*Channing Jeschke unpacks one of almost ten thousand cartons of books shipped from Hartford to Candler in 1976.*

Despite these challenges, by the time he retired in 1994—at the end of Candler's eightieth year—Jeschke had polished nearly every facet of what could arguably be called the most brilliant jewel in the research crown of Emory.

A worthy successor to Jeschke was not difficult to find. One of the hallmarks of the Pitts Theology Library in the past thirty years has been its preparation of librarians to take the top positions at theology libraries around the country—at Iliff School of Theology, Hartford Theological Seminary, Columbia Theological Seminary, Union Seminary in New York, and Harvard Divinity School, among others. There seemed to be no reason to make Pitts an exception to the list of theology schools clamoring for its librarians.

Close at hand, to succeed as the Margaret A. Pitts Professor of Theological Bibliography and director of the library, was Matt Patrick Graham, the reference librarian. Graham had earned his PhD in Old Testament studies from Emory in 1983, then had gone off to teach in Oregon and Texas while also earning a library degree. He returned to Candler as a catalog librarian in 1988 and had learned the full range of operations at Pitts under Jeschke's leadership.

The next twenty years witnessed astonishing changes in the way libraries serve their constituencies. Thank the Internet. The early excursions into web-based cataloguing of library resources at Emory had begun just before Graham's advent to Pitts, with the installation of an off-the-shelf information management system called DOBIS/LIBIS, which Emory tailored to its own specifications. This system required barcoding every document in the Emory libraries—and, of course, installing the equipment to read the barcodes, which led to more budget balancing.

As Y2K—the year 2000—loomed, millennial fears prompted preparations for possible digital doom: early computer programmers had failed to foresee the need for

**MERTON COLLECTION**   In collaboration with the Aquinas Center at Emory, Pitts Theology Library has built a modest collection of early editions of the works of Thomas Merton and has digitized more than fifty of his manuscript notebooks housed at the Merton Center at Bellarmine University.

computer records to contain four-digit rather than two-digit figures for years. Information technology throughout the university received a thorough scrubbing as well as doses of digital growth hormones. By 2000 the new online library system at Emory had been dubbed EUCLID, and Pitts was a full participant. Pitts also had its own information technology department and had undertaken major projects to make rare materials available digitally. The first of these projects was the Pitts Digital Image Archive, which in 2000–2001 made twenty-three hundred images available online, most of them from the sixteenth century. This archive continues to grow each year and by 2013 was approaching fifty thousand images.

In 2008, librarians began creating online research guides to the collection. With funding from the Lilly Endowment the library also assumed responsibility for assisting faculty in the use of technology in teaching, and in time the theology school would turn to the library IT department for support of all academic and administrative computing in the school. Pitts contributed to the substantial iTunes U holdings at Emory, beginning with Reformation Day programs and exhibitions of rare materials in the display cases in Pitts. Volunteers used flatbed scanners and digital cameras to make even more materials available online—fifty-five hundred exposures in the first year alone (2010–11).

Even as the whirring, beeping, and glimmering of the most advanced technology infiltrated the library, patrons continued to voice old-fashioned complaints: the lighting was poor, the furniture worn, access difficult, the stacks jammed. The roof still leaked. Mold still grew. The university, taking note, prepared to open a new theology library in 2014, at the centennial of Candler's founding.

*Cardinal Manning played a crucial role in the promulgation of the doctrine of papal infallibility by the First Vatican Council in 1870. This draft of the doctrine, in Manning's hand, is part of the Manning Collection in Pitts Library.*

*Cannon Chapel presents a humane scale rather than looming over Rudolph Courtyard.*

## CHAPTER EIGHT

# ARTS, RIGHTS, BOOM, AND CHANGE

OF all the decades that might serve as candidates for a golden era, the 1970s were not one. The longer they hung around, the more they seemed to show that the country, the university, and the seminary all had reasons for anxiety about the future.

On the national scene, the hard-fought presidential campaign in 1976 resulted in a narrow victory by a former Georgia governor named Jimmy Carter and offered the hope of moving on from the Watergate legacy of Richard Nixon and the turmoil of the Vietnam War, which had ended finally the previous year. Yet by 1978 an energy crisis, double-digit inflation, and rising unemployment began to shake confidence in the nation's ability to reclaim the robust growth and optimism of the early 1960s.

In higher education, the mid-1970s brought a dawning realization that if colleges and universities had ever experienced a golden age, it probably began to close around 1970. Federal research dollars were declining; jobs for PhD graduates (especially in the humanities, the historic foundation for theological study and ministry) were in desperately short supply; faculty morale generally was slipping; and the national image of campuses had never quite recovered from the pictures of anger and violence at Columbia, Berkeley, and Kent State.

On seminary campuses, likewise, changes set in motion during the previous two decades—through the civil rights movement and the antiwar movement— led to transformation of the student body, not always without tension. Although

When Jimmy Carter joined the Emory faculty as University Distinguished Professor in 1982, Dean Waits began serving for two years as interim executive director of The Carter Center.

women had been granted elders orders by Methodist denominations as early as 1880, ordination of women was uncommon until the 1950s, and most mainline denominations were slow to adopt the practice (1970, for instance, for the Evangelical Lutheran Church in America, and 1974 for the Episcopal Church). By 1977, however, nearly 18 percent of Candler students were women, most of them studying for the MDiv. Similarly, although Emory University won the right to integrate only in 1962, within fifteen years the student body at Candler was 6 percent black, despite the presence in Atlanta of the historically African American Interdenominational Theological Center (including the United Methodist Gammon Seminary).

Thus, in the spring of 1977, when the Emory board of trustees tapped the dean of the theology school, Jim Laney, to become the next president of the university, Candler faced the need for someone who could help the seminary engage immediately with rapid changes without missing a step, and without losing sight of the vision that Laney had inspired—the vision of a nationally preeminent school of theology that educated ministers for the church and scholars for the academy (perhaps also scholars for the ministry and ministers for the academy). Fortunately the newly appointed president was able to turn to his associate dean, Jim Waits, and pass the baton to him.

Waits had come to Candler from Nashville along with Laney in 1969. Born in 1935 in Mississippi, Waits earned degrees from Millsaps College and Yale Divinity School before earning his MA in political science from the University of Chicago. As a member of the Mississippi Conference of the Methodist Church, in January 1963 he joined twenty-seven other Methodist clergy in issuing the Born of Conviction statement. Half a century after its publication, the statement appears gentle and moderate, yet it generated much heat at the time. In the statement, the twenty-eight clergy expressed concern about the social crises brought about by "racial discord" and by the threat to close public schools rather than integrate them. Affirming their belief in the church as "the instrument of God's purpose" and their adherence to the social principles of the Methodist Church regarding the "brotherhood" of all races, the men quietly and briefly reminded the church of certain foundational truths, while also declaring their belief in the indispensable value of public schools as a means for preserving and strengthening democracy. Finally, for good measure, the clergy clarified the distinction between the civil rights movement and communism. While they affirmed their support of the former, they agreed with the Methodist Church in opposing the latter as inimical to the Lordship of Christ.

Mailed to *The New York Times* as well as newspapers around the state, the statement drew censure, death threats, and harassment to the signatories. The risks could not be minimized; this was three months after segregationists rioted at the University of Mississippi to protest the enrollment of James Meredith there, and six months before the assassination of Medgar Evars. Waits, one of four coauthors of the statement, soon left Mississippi to pursue graduate study. He later found an appointment as associate pastor at West End Methodist Church in Nashville, and while in Nashville he met James Laney in 1967. Two years later, having developed a personal rapport and professional respect for Waits's abilities and commitments, Laney invited him to come along to Candler and join the administration.

After eight years as Laney's assistant and later associate dean (stepping in to fill Mack Stokes's role when he was elected bishop in 1972), Waits was deeply familiar with the makeup and operations of the school. He also knew quite well the new

D. W. Brooks, for whom Brooks Commons in Cannon Chapel was named, turns a shovel of sod at the ground-breaking for the chapel on August 30, 1979. Joining him in regalia are (left to right) President Jimmy Carter, Emory Board Chair Henry L. Bowden, Emory Trustee O. Wayne Rollins, and Bishop William R. Cannon. Jack Gilbert, director of development for Candler at the time, is handing a shovel to Bishop Cannon.

leader of the university, President Laney. That did not make him an automatic choice to become permanent dean. He served for a year as acting dean while a search was under way, but in the end the search committee found its best prospect already in the dean's office in Bishops Hall.

Waits's knowledge of the school and the university president certainly made it easier for him to address the challenges at Candler immediately, in a way that someone from outside Candler might not have done. The challenges were serious. The seminary was bursting at the seams, as its largest enrollment in history brought 601 students to Bishops Hall in the fall of 1977, a 40 percent growth in the student body in the eight years of Laney's deanship, matched by a 28 percent growth in the faculty. Fully 15 percent of these students hailed from beyond the Southeast and represented a measure of Candler's growing national

visibility and stature. While there was much to celebrate, the strain on facilities and on the faculty was terrific.

Difficult in another way was the stress on community in the theology school as plans took shape for a new chapel. Since the transformation of Durham Chapel into a reference room for the Pitts Theology Library two years earlier, both Candler and the university had made do with ad hoc attempts to continue their worship life. The regular worship services of Candler were held in the attic of Bishops Hall, and those of University Worship (an ecumenical Protestant service presided over by the university chaplain every Sunday morning) were held in a small, auditorium-style classroom in the Sociology Building (now Carlos Hall). One of the conditions placed on Candler by the university administration when the Theology Building was renovated for library use was that the theology school must build an alternative to Durham Chapel as a place for teaching and worship.

At the end of a decade of global anxiety, budgetary constraint, and social change, the prospect of channeling several million dollars into an edifice did not sit well with some members of the theology community. Many students in particular pointed to the need for greater community building between the university and the city, and they suggested that more faithful discipleship called for diverting the funds for the chapel into programs of service instead. Waits would later call the ensuing community debate about the issue "an extended and searching discussion concerning [the] theological justification and need" for a new chapel. In many ways this discussion reflected the community dynamics that had become one of Candler's hallmarks over the decades—as a place where deeply held but often divergent theological convictions could be expressed without damage to the school's fundamental unity of vision and hope.

As the debate continued, planning started. Necessary to satisfy part of the teaching function of the seminary, the chapel had to offer versatility for different forms of worship as well as universality in welcoming non-Christian religious groups. Professor Theodore Weber, as chapel pastor at Candler, offered theological perspectives on how the space should be designed; Professor Don Saliers helped guide thinking about the liturgical uses of the space (including dance and drama); Professor Harry Moon offered acoustical advice.

Paul Rudolph—the dean of the school of architecture at Yale, whose father had been Candler's first graduate back in 1915—presented his initial design in January 1977 for review by students and faculty. The outcome could not have made him happy. His presentation prompted dismay in some quarters and led to

Jimmy Carter, the first U.S. president to visit the Emory campus, speaks at the ground-breaking ceremony for Cannon Chapel. To his left are Emory president James T. Laney and executive vice president Judson C. "Jake" Ward.

three public forums in the winter of 1978 (including one with Rudolph himself). In March 1978 the Coalition Against the Chapel organized itself to protest chapel developments. In response, Waits appointed a Student Advisory Committee to consult with the Chapel Building Committee.

Two months later, on May 29, a committee of faculty and students issued a document titled "Theological and Historical Statements concerning the Proposed Chapel Complex." "Who could foresee," the statement said, "that a facility intended to enhance the quality of communal life at Candler would generate conditions ripe for dissent and division? Yet, such a time confronts us, and our response to these conditions manifests the quality of our life together. We believe these statements to be hope–full signs that at once express and intend community."

The document was signed by faculty members James Hopewell, Channing Jeschke, James May, Theodore Runyon, Jim Waits, and Theodore Weber, along with students Mike Cavin, John Dorris, Frances Guest, Dan Howell, Sara Phillips, Tina Pippin, John Powers, and Tim Smiley.

The theological statement noted concerns about the privilege, security, and affluence of the university community as a consequence of "the present politico-economic structure of the world . . . [We enjoy] a community life wrought by our society in part through its opportunism and oppression." Practicing good pulpit rhetoric, the statement went on, "In this inequity we may share, while others are deprived; we may sing, while others sob; we may care, while others suffer; we may study, while others lose their humanity; we may reconcile, while others are alienated; we may eat, while others starve."

"Pervasive guilt" and "ambiguity" were an inescapable part of "being a Christian in America today." To address this ambiguity, the theological statement pointed out that the new chapel would enable faith to be lived out concretely, through meeting and worship, not merely in intellectual abstraction. The chapel would serve as an intersection of "all the paths of community life." The new space offered possibilities for "witness within the university, mission within the seminary, and renewal within the Church."

Regarding the first possibility, the report noted the effectiveness of old Durham Chapel in "witnessing to the centrality of faith in the life of the University." This witness, the report suggested, must be replaced. Regarding the second possibility, of work within the seminary, the report said the meetinghouse would "work no magical communion" but would be space in which to support transformation of "a largely self-serving collectivity of students and staff into a fellowship of the Spirit."

Paul Rudolph designed the interior of Cannon Chapel to reveal the structure of the building.

Finally, the report noted potential for the new space to offer opportunities for imaginative experimenting and reshaping of community in worship, thus holding out models for renewal of the life of the broader church. The report even put forth the prospect that the new chapel would influence building plans of graduates as they entered into ministry—as, apparently, Durham Chapel had done.

Soon the community was resolved to go forward, and general agreement reigned among students and faculty about the direction of the chapel's development. Greater dissatisfaction seemed to reside in the architect. Rudolph proposed an altar table whose shape the advisory committee rejected; he fumed. Rudolph proposed painting gray the beautiful natural wood of the Holtkamp pipe organ, and the organ designer refused; Rudolph fumed.

In the end, the project moved inexorably toward completion. The university broke ground for the chapel on August 30, 1979, as President Laney and Dean Waits presided over a ceremony in which U.S. president Jimmy Carter spoke, Bishop Cannon joined others in turning a shovel full of dirt, and participants bore up under the intolerable heat of academic regalia in the middle of an Atlanta summer.

(The association between Waits and Carter would continue, for when President Carter accepted appointment as University Distinguished Professor at Emory in 1982 and began planning development of what became the Carter Center, Waits was appointed to serve part-time as director of the incipient nongovernmental organization, a job he would fill for two years.)

Meanwhile, the development of a strong academic program continued apace. In the same academic year of the chapel debate, 1977–78, a task force recommended changing the seminary calendar to the semester system, a recommendation approved unanimously by the Candler faculty. The change meant that students and faculty both would conclude their academic year before the onslaught of Methodist annual conference meetings. The change from the quarter system also offered a more measured pace for deeper study and would accommodate cross-registration within the university—for instance, in developing dual-degree programs with the schools of law and business. The only foreseeable difficulty—that the graduate school would stay on the quarter system and complicate life for the Graduate Division of Religion—was averted when the entire university moved to semesters in 1982.

Within the faculty itself, Waits enlarged upon Laney's initial pursuit of

*Noel Erskine arrived at Candler in 1978 as assistant professor of theology and ethics.*

eminence and diversity. The leading Methodist Church hymnist, Carlton (Sam) Young, joined the faculty in the fall of 1978, and Roberta Chesnut (later Bondi) arrived in the fall of 1979 to be the first woman appointed to a tenured position at Candler. As Waits noted in his annual report that year, her appointment helped fulfill one of the goals of affirmative action "without compromising standards of excellence and scholarly competence." The following year, Waits scored a coup in homiletics with the appointment of Fred Craddock as professor of preaching, and the dean strengthened three different areas of study by appointing Luther Smith (church and community), Steve Tipton (sociology of religion), and Carol Newsom (Old Testament).

By the end of his second year as dean, Waits could write without reservation, "There simply is no theological faculty in America that rivals them in the unique combination of scholarship, dedication to the profession of ministry, and creativity that characterizes this one." That year Nancy Hardesty, a visiting professor, was teaching feminist theology of Rosemary Radford Reuther and Mary Daly; Clinton Gardner was teaching biomedical ethics; Noel Erskine was teaching black theology and ethics and team teaching a course with Ted Runyon on theologies of hope and liberation (focusing on eschatology and the apocalypse in Moltmann, Teilhard, and Latin American theology); Don Saliers was developing his distinctive profile in liturgical theology by blending linguistic philosophies, aesthetics, and liturgics; Leander Keck was teaching New Testament anthropology and "Christology of the Lives of Jesus."

Winds of change were blowing in the school. In June 1979 the composition of the faculty was 90 percent male, 10 percent female, and 5 percent black. In addition to twenty-eight United Methodists, the faculty included four Episcopalians, two Roman Catholics, two Baptists, and one each from Presbyterian, Christian Methodist Episcopalian, Disciples, United Church of Christ, and Dutch Reformed denominations. Some 85 percent were ordained.

More significantly, changes to the student body went hand in hand with changes in the curriculum, as increasing attention to liberation and feminist theologies both precipitated and followed the increasing numbers of female and African American students. Again, as in the debate over the chapel, such change did not come without a degree of friction in the community. Echoing the experience of the wider university a decade earlier, following the admission of African American students especially to the college, Candler woke up to the awareness that admitting a new class of students is not the same as making a place for them in the community. (In the university, the Black Student Alliance had called attention to the isolation felt by the still small number of black students in a predominantly white institution, and had advocated for better programming for advising, mentoring, and building community among minority students.) Although the faculty and administration of Candler supported and aggressively sought increased diversity in the student body, the Candler community wrestled with questions about the appropriate role of the Black Student Caucus, about the best way for the curriculum to address the needs of women and minorities, and the question of faculty appointments that would be both representative of and

By 1991, when this photograph was taken in front of the Turner Conference Center in Jim Waits's last year as dean, the Candler faculty had changed significantly in both size and diversity.

conducive to the school's demographic transformation.

Perhaps most indicative of the level of theological and pedagogical commitments of the faculty was a program known as the Common Program Seminars, or CP400. Inaugurated during the Cannon administration with the beginning of the Graduate Division of Religion, these seminars persisted into the Waits administration. Their intention was to bring together, in weekly seminars, graduate students in at least their second year of the PhD program with faculty members who taught in the GDR regardless of their tenure home—whether in the various college departments of religion, sociology, or political science or in the school of theology itself. Each year of seminars was organized around a theme. Each week a faculty member would issue a paper beforehand, in time for participants to read it, and the seminar session would begin with a graduate student's ten-minute response to the paper followed by full-bore discussion.

Bill Mallard kept copious records of each year's series of CP400 seminars. In 1961–62 the theme was eschatology, with papers presented by the eminent philosopher Charles Hartshorne (then at Emory College); Gregor Sebba and

*Maestro Robert Shaw, conductor of the Atlanta Symphony Orchestra from 1967 until 1988, accepted appointment as Robert W. Woodruff Professor at Emory in 1989. Several times during his tenure he conducted the Candler Choraliers, who had achieved national stature under the direction of Assistant Professor Steven Darsey (in white shirt and bow tie).*

Walter Strauss (both then in the Institute for Liberal Arts); Norman Perrin, Ted Weber, and Mallard from the theology school; and others from the college. In 1968 Weber, Jürgen Moltmann, William Beardslee, Thomas Altizer, and Vincent Harding (then at Spelman College) gave papers on the theme "Revolution and Christian Responsibility." Five years later, it was Sebba, Justo Gonzalez, James Gouinlock (philosophy), and Jackson Carroll and Clinton Gardner of the theology school leading the discussions on "Authority: Its Sources and Functions." In 1975–76, in a series on "Nature and Grace: The Crisis of Contemporary Freedom," Charles Gerkin wrote from a pastoral counselor's perspective on a delinquent gang, Gardner wrote about medical experimentation with human subjects, David Smith (in the Sociology Department of Emory College) wrote on sin and society, and Kenneth Anderson (from the Anatomy Department of the School of Medicine) wrote on decision making in experimental medicine.

*Romney Moseley, on Candler's faculty from 1981 to 1989, served as assistant dean and associate director of the Center for Faith Development, where he applied the dialectics of Kierkegaard to the study of moral and faith development while working with James Fowler.*

The fruits of CP400 were many, but perhaps greatest were the influence of the school of theology in leavening the intellectual fiber of the humanities at Emory, the mentorships nurtured and strengthened between graduate faculty and graduate students, and the sense of collegiality that allowed participants to challenge intellectual positions while respecting each other's good faith and integrity.

To attend to the important work of development and nurturing of church relations, Waits hired Jack Gilbert, a Pennsylvania native and ordained Methodist clergyman, who brought to the work of fund-raising both a deft personal touch and professional experience that ratcheted up Candler's achievements in this area. He also blended high intelligence with an imaginative sense of fun. Gilbert set the bar high, and in time his effectiveness led to his appointment to positions of greater responsibility in the central university advancement office before his retirement in 2000. The work of Gilbert and his small staff was critical to raising money for faculty research, as well as to the remarkable growth in endowment for student scholarships. Possessed of a great talent for developing rapport with members of the church, Gilbert also played a vital part in nurturing a closer relationship between Candler and United Methodist constituencies.

The engine of theological education appeared to be running smoothly in the

Druid Hills section of Atlanta—a faculty of growing reputation, good staff in place, solid enrollment and income—when suddenly in November 1979 the university announced a change to higher octane of sorts. The brothers Woodruff—Robert and George—were transferring to Emory the entire corpus of their parents' estate, worth $105 million. At the time, the gift was the largest ever to any institution of higher education in America. At Emory the momentous announcement set off a yearlong, intense self-study at all levels and in every school and college.

For Candler, the year of self-scrutiny included a helpful review of administrative organization as well as an assessment of learning—how students were engaging with critical methods of scholarship, how the school and churches were gauging students' readiness for professional life, and how the faculty were undertaking their own professional development. (The Lilly Endowment funded both the administrative and the student assessments.) Much of the year of self-study aimed at considering how Candler should minister to the emerging needs of the church in the 1980s. One significant outgrowth of all this assessment was the institution of a process for faculty evaluation that stressed the importance of effective teaching in theological education. This process would become, within another decade or so, the model for faculty evaluation throughout the university.

Spurred by the jolt of energy that the Woodruff gift brought to the university, Candler enjoyed a decade of tremendous growth and vitality during the 1980s. The school launched programs in Methodist and ecumenical studies, under the direction of Professor Theodore Runyon, and an Episcopal Studies Program under the direction of Professor Theodore Hackett, building on the Experiment in Ministry program established with the Atlanta Episcopal Diocese in 1972. Other institutes and centers established during the decade included the Institute for World Evangelism, the Center for Research in Faith and Moral Development directed by James W. Fowler III, and the Black Church Studies Program founded by Robert Franklin (later president of Morehouse College, and still later professor in the James T. and Berta R. Laney Chair of Moral Leadership). Joint-degree programs linked the theology school with the schools of business and law.

In addition to new programming, the school attracted a raft of celebrated scholars as visiting faculty members: José Miguez Bonino, Jürgen Moltmann, C. K. Barrett, Elizabeth Moltmann-Wendell. Again, these appointments significantly enhanced Candler's offerings in Latin American liberation theology, feminist theology, and the theology of hope, all of which engaged Candler's faculty in constructive ways. Ted Runyon, for instance, expanded his role as an interpreter of

European theology for the American church by writing of Wesley in part from a perspective provided by Moltmann. A list of visiting lecturers during the decade reads like a who's who in American theology: Mary Daly, Don Browning, Letty Russell, John Cobb, Julian Hartt, Brevard Childs, James Gustafson.

Along with these somewhat traditional advances toward eminence, Dean Waits led Candler in exploring the role of the arts in theology, worship, and religious life. Nothing exemplified this interest of his more than the first year of programming in Cannon Chapel. The opening of the chapel in September 1981 made room for a flourishing of the arts in the midst of the seminary community. In addition to 304 liturgical events, that first year in the chapel witnessed 68 concerts, 169 class

Archbishop Desmond Tutu (shown here with Provost Billy Frye and Candler dean Jim Waits) began his association with Emory when he delivered the commencement address and received an honorary degree in 1988. He later served two terms (1991 and 1998-2000) as Visiting Robert W. Woodruff Professor at Candler.

sessions, 9 conferences, 17 lectures and poetry readings, 14 noon recitals, 5 master classes, 16 weddings, and assorted rehearsals and organ lessons—all attended by a cumulative total of nearly fifty-six thousand persons. Even the courtyard was used heavily for concerts, honor ceremonies, square dances, picnics, and a barbecue dinner. Most gratifying to some, in view of the commitments of the earlier theological statement about the chapel, the year of activities included two consultations on mission—one on the future of the black church and one titled "Poverty and Dependence in America."

Faculty, too, were leading the school and the university in boldly stepping out on the international stage. Spurred by the theology faculty's interest in human rights, the university agreed to sponsor a yearlong program titled "Re-thinking Human Rights." Cochaired by David Pacini, who was then a junior faculty member, the year culminated in a symposium that brought to the Emory campus such eminent scholars and thinkers as David Tracy, Leszek Kolakowski, Dieter Henrich, and Maurice Cranston. The American Academy of Arts and Sciences devoted an entire

*During Ministers' Week in January 1983, part of a yearlong focus on human rights at Emory, the university conferred honorary degrees on three notables. Shown here with Candler dean Jim Waits and Emory president James Laney are United Methodist bishop Earl Hunt, Nobel Prize laureate Elie Wiesel, and United Methodist bishop James Armstrong.*

issue of its journal, *Daedalus*, to proceedings of the symposium.

With so much new programming under way, and despite vigorous fund-raising, the budget was beginning to experience strain. During Waits's first five years as dean, the operating budget of the school doubled from $2 million to $4 million. Charging higher tuition than other United Methodist seminaries, the school was competing also with divinity schools at Harvard, Yale, and Princeton, where faculty salaries were higher. At the same time, the central university administration was beginning to withdraw its means of propping up the Candler budget, and The United Methodist Church changed its formula for distributing the Ministerial Education Fund, thus decreasing contributions from the church. Bishops Hall needed attention, the community longed for a residential center and on-campus housing, and Pitts Library had to overcome a deficit in collections to support doctoral-level scholarship. The need for new funding sources was clear.

With this in mind, Waits and the administration planned a campaign to raise endowment and capital funds. The Campaign for Emory, which had brought in the munificent Woodruff gift in 1979, was a university-wide campaign that had supported schools and programs throughout the university. Much of that campaign's final tally of $220 million was unrestricted endowment funds, and little of it was earmarked for the theology school. Thus, even before the university completed the Campaign for Emory in 1984, Candler launched its own campaign in 1982 with a goal of raising $8.5 million specifically for the theology school. The five-year campaign achieved its goal ahead of schedule and closed with $12 million by the end of fiscal year 1988. The funds supported scholarships, faculty chairs, the library, and—importantly—development of a complex on Clifton Road that would open in 1989. Called Turner Village, the project entailed construction of a small conference center and the renovation of old apartment buildings near the current Emory Conference Center Hotel. The complex would serve the theology school for nearly twenty years before the university razed Turner Village to make room for Emory Point.

Throughout the decade, Waits and the faculty sought out and recruited a remarkable number of women faculty members who would excel both at Emory and, in many cases, in the academy beyond. They included Carol Ann Newsom, an expert on the Dead Sea Scrolls and later a Charles Howard Candler Professor at Candler; Nancy Ammerman, who would launch the Baptist Studies Program and was commissioned to write the principal report on the U.S. government's

*Luther Smith, a faculty member since 1979, would become one of four Candler professors to serve as president of the Emory University Senate from 1987 to 2004.*

mismanagement of the Branch Davidian conflict in 1992; Jane Dammen McAuliffe, the first scholar of Islam at Candler and later president of Bryn Mawr College; Rebecca Chopp, a systematic theologian and feminist scholar, who would become the first female provost of Emory and, later, president of Colgate University and Swarthmore College; and Gail R. O'Day, Shatford Professor of Preaching and later dean of the Wake Forest School of Divinity.

The composition of the faculty underwent dramatic transformation in just three years, between fall 1986 and fall 1989, as the appointment of eleven full-time, tenure-track faculty added five women, one African American, and one Asian to the roster of distinguished scholars.

No less dramatic was the transformation of the student body during this decade. By 1989, fully 46 percent of the entering class were older than thirty, and 21 percent were older than forty, as an increasing number of second-career students pushed the median age of the student body well beyond the traditional postcollegiate years. Women made up 32 percent of those entering; 23 percent of the entering students were underrepresented minorities. Half of the students were married, a third with children, and all of the students had greater financial needs than students just five or ten years previously. Three-fourths of them worked. Despite the financial pressures, student morale was, in Waits's view, remarkably high, with students "generating involvements and seizing opportunities for service"—for example, in planning a weeklong conference on spirituality and peacemaking, developing forums on care of the earth, reconstituting the Women's Caucus, and launching Women's Emphasis Week.

In the fall of 1989, as Candler turned seventy-five years old, the school planned a spate of birthday celebrations, from the Richard C. Kessler Concert in October to extended anniversary observances in the spring, with a historical exhibit in the Schatten Gallery of Woodruff Library and events exploring the importance of arts to ministry and theological education.

The real celebration of the maturing of Candler, however, came in sundry other ways. One was the launching of the Black Church Studies Program "to educate and heighten the awareness of the entire Candler community regarding the origins, development, contemporary diversity, and genius of the black church tradition."

Similarly, the appointment of the first part-time director of the new Women's Studies Program, Kris Kvam, who began her work in the fall of 1990, made it plain that Candler now sought to understand more fully the role of women in ministry.

Moreover, while Candler was branching out with initiatives like these, it also reaffirmed its traditional roots by making "demonstrated competence in preaching" a curricular requirement for the MDiv. No one would leave Candler unfit for the pulpit. Indeed, the Teaching Parish Program—another signature of Candler's commitment to training students for ministry—had expanded its reach, and five United Methodist annual conferences now required their Candler students who were working in parishes to enroll in the program.

In the spring of 1991, following a remarkable era of vitality in the school, Waits resigned the deanship to accept the position of executive director of the Association of Theological Schools in the United States and Canada. For the

**JIM WAITS'S PRAYER**    In his final meeting with the Candler faculty, in May 1991 Jim Waits opened with this prayer, which gives a sense of his own calling and that of the school to faithful leadership and devoted service.

*O Eternal God, who has gathered this community of scholars and teachers to serve your purpose these many years; You who have endowed them with the rich heritage of learning; who have given them the vocations of rightly discerning the sacred things: we rejoice in our gathering today and in the mystery of all gifts you have bestowed upon this very special community.*

*We bring to you this day, O Lord, our joy, our suffering, the satisfactions and ambiguities of our calling. Make us aware of the sheer abundance of our life together, and of the stark needs of your world's people. Quicken our consciousness wherever there is oppression or injustice of any kind, even among ourselves. And make us always sturdy advocates of the good.*

*Bless the new leadership of this community, O God; inspire it with vision and sustain it with the rich colleagueship which abides here. And lead us, both now and in the future, to please you and to seek to fulfill your purposes in all that we say and do. In the name of Christ, our Lord, we pray.*

previous two years he had been guiding a Lilly Endowment–funded study of university-related schools of theology, and that, along with his two decades of experience in theology schools, fitted him admirably to the work of envisioning the role of theological education in the coming decade.

In his last annual report as dean, Waits foreshadowed difficulties that would continue to occupy the thinking and energy of the Candler administration. After reaching a peak of 502 full-time-equivalent (FTE) students in 1988 (and a high head count of 660 in 1987), enrollment in the fall of 1990 had dropped to 455 FTE; entering MDiv students numbered 101, down sharply from 144 two years earlier.

In addition to concerns about enrollment, the budget continued to be a source of worry. Tuition accounted for 53 percent of the budget, meaning that any slip in enrollment could have damaging consequences to operations. Moreover, tuition at Candler cost fully a thousand dollars more than the next most expensive United Methodist seminary, making recruitment a challenge. While Candler attracted significant grants, none of that money supported the teaching and operations of the school. (For instance, the Lilly Endowment provided $638,000 over three years to examine student faith and the practices of Christian congregations, a project directed by Associate Professor Thomas Frank and involving six other faculty members.) Although Candler led all schools and divisions at Emory in pledges and contributions received from a Coca-Cola challenge grant during the Emory fund-raising campaign of 1990–95, those funds did not go into the endowment and thus did not result in a steady, reliable source of income from investments. During his last year, Waits sought to reduce the budget by $300,000 to offset tuition shortfall from underenrollment. He called these efforts "frustrating and counterproductive," unless the school planned for general downsizing, which in turn would erode the "quality and character" of the teaching and curriculum.

Despite these evident challenges for his successor, Waits concluded his last report by remarking on the Candler faculty, which he described as "magnificent both in its quality and in its humaneness. Its devotion to the Church is comprised of deep faithfulness as well as a profound understanding of the Church's humanity." This faculty would carry the school to still greater heights in the challenging decade ahead.

*Cannon Chapel as it appears from White Hall at night.*

*Turner Conference Center served as the anchor for Turner Village.*

## CHAPTER NINE

# FORWARD THROUGH RETRENCHMENT AND "CULTURE WARS"

IN April 1991 Emory president James Laney visited the monthly meeting of the Candler faculty—of which he was, still, technically a member—to poll the assembled faculty members on the recommended choice of a new dean.

Almost unanimously, the thirty-nine voting faculty supported the appointment of R. Kevin LaGree. The one abstention and one no vote were anonymous and unexplained, but they may have had to do with the path LaGree took to the deanship. The search committee, chaired by the distinguished church historian Brooks Holifield, had recommended appointment of someone without a scholarly publication on his curriculum vitae or a single year anywhere as a full-time faculty member.

After graduating with distinction and honors in history from the University of Kansas in 1971, LaGree had gone off to Harvard Law School to earn a JD and begin a career in law; he had risen in time to the corporate legal department of Hallmark Cards, in Kansas City, Missouri. Before long, however, he felt called to the ministry, and in 1980 he graduated with an honors MDiv from Saint Paul School of Theology. His quick intelligence and affability soon led to his appointment at First United Methodist Church in Topeka. Along the way, he taught briefly as an adjunct faculty member at Saint Paul and served that seminary for two years as vice president for institutional advancement.

Still—despite his evident intellectual capabilities and his experience in administrative leadership—the Candler School of Theology had moved well beyond the time when the appointment of a churchman without solid academic credentials, like Burton Trimble or Jim Waits, could be viewed as the academic dean without some reservation. Waits himself had had years of experience teaching and administering the school before becoming dean, and he had come to share responsibility for the academic development of the school with associate deans Carl Holladay and Jane McAuliffe, both of whom had international scholarly reputations.

*Kevin LaGree served as dean of Candler from 1991 until 1999.*

LaGree would later comment that he viewed his appointment as dean, "directly from the senior pastorate of a church," as evidence of the commitment of the faculty and the university to "the school's mutuality with the church." He noted that while the choice was a rarity among university-based seminaries, "where chief executive officers tend to [be] drawn from the ranks of faculty," LaGree saw the selection of a pastor to be dean as fitting for a school from which 80 percent of its graduates went on to serve as local pastors, and whose alumni included at that time nine active bishops.

At that same faculty meeting in 1991, Emory provost Billy Frye announced that the university would smooth the transition for the new dean by absorbing the $2 million accumulated deficit that burdened the school (when the budget for Candler in fiscal year 1991 was $7.45 million). In addition, the university would put up three hundred thousand dollars to enhance recruitment of students in the face of declining enrollment.

The faculty greeted Frye's good news with applause. Frye went on, however, to note that the new dean would have to lead an assessment of the scope and number of programs and activities in the school in order to reverse the untenable combination of overspending and lower revenues. Two consultants who had visited Candler independently in the spring (Jackson Forstman, dean of Vanderbilt Divinity School, and Anthony Ruger, a senior research fellow at Auburn Theological Seminary) both had made recommendations to address the school's needs. The first recommendation was to create a committee to address long-range faculty development and fiscal matters, and the second was to begin strategic planning around student recruitment, admissions, and financial aid. Additionally, Forstman had commented on what he termed "a dispersion of efforts of faculty," who were spread thin across too many programs. All of these issues would be imperatives for the new dean to address right away.

As if to signal a new regimen of austerity, Dean LaGree announced in August at his first faculty retreat that the usual list of recent faculty publications, customarily distributed individually to all faculty members at the monthly faculty meetings, henceforth would be kept in a binder in the dean's office for faculty to consult at their leisure—thus reducing the use and cost of paper. (To some, this also signaled, symbolically, a diminishment of the school's priority on scholarship.) Similarly, the school would no longer pick up the tab for the faculty lunches that used to follow the monthly faculty meetings; these would become, for a time, "self-funded," and a number of faculty members began a brown-bag practice.

Other notes sounded at the retreat also suggested a sharpened attention to the regularization of policies and procedures. For the sake of tracking and recouping costs as well as asserting control over its own facilities, the school now would require any non-Candler groups or organizations wanting to use its buildings—Bishops Hall, Cannon Chapel, or Turner Village—to make reservations through Auxiliary Services. This policy would allow the school to charge for any extraordinary cleanup or other costs.

At the retreat LaGree acknowledged with appreciation the several faculty members who had taught summer school without compensation in 1991, and he hoped that such sacrifice would not be necessary in the future. Meanwhile, the development office would look into the possibility that the faculty members could claim their contributed teaching time as a tax-deductible gift to Candler.

While financial and programmatic matters loomed large at this first meeting of the new dean with his faculty, one faculty member sounded an alarm that would reverberate throughout the near decade of LaGree's deanship and require much of his attention and energy. Rebecca Chopp commented on the growing concern among United Methodist seminaries and colleges about the Good News Movement, part of the Confessing Movement of conservative voices in mainline Protestant denominations. Since 1967 the Good News organization had worked actively to call Methodism back to what the movement viewed as orthodox Wesleyan belief and practice, especially with regard to the importance of evangelism and the exclusion of homosexuals from ecclesial authority. One of the leading lights of the movement was Maxie Dunnam, longtime editor of the *Upper Room* and a Candler alumnus (1958).

To the extent that the Good News Movement viewed declining membership in mainline Protestantism as an outgrowth of heterodoxy, or a turning from the true path, the movement laid the blame at the threshold of many of the older Methodist seminaries. Chopp observed in that August retreat that many of the seminaries and schools feared the movement would attempt to infiltrate their boards of trustees, much as conservative Southern Baptists had done through the 1980s, essentially wresting control of the Southern Baptist educational structure from more moderate Baptists and further splintering that denomination.

This concern over the appropriate or desirable levels of influence between theological conservatism and theological progressivism—a debate harking back to the first decade of Candler's history and continuing through debates over integration and "the death of God"—would pervade LaGree's years as dean and affect a range of concerns in the school, from fund-raising to the awarding of scholarships to use of Cannon Chapel to the recruitment and retention of students. In a real sense, theology and administration became entwined, and both the Candler faculty and the wider university community would in turn become entangled in these matters.

By the end of his first year, LaGree had made significant strides toward carrying out the charge given to him by the Emory administration—a charge that was essentially a mandate to get the school sailing on an even keel financially. Wisely, he enlisted the faculty in developing a mission statement for the school to help set future directions and goals. Aiming to reduce expenses, he set forth a five-year financial plan intended to bring the budget into equilibrium by the 1995–96 academic year.

To enhance student recruitment, LaGree received permission from the administration to freeze tuition at Candler at the 1991–92 level for the following year, and he hired Mary Lou Greenwood Boice as assistant dean for admissions and student services. To free himself for the important work of connecting the school more firmly to the church and undertaking significant development activities— essentially going on the road for chicken dinners in every United Methodist fellowship hall in the Southeastern Jurisdiction and then some—he appointed Carl

*Archbishop Desmond Tutu and José Miguez Bonino, both Visiting Woodruff Professors at Candler, engaged in conversation during a symposium in front of the fireplace at the Turner Conference Center.*

Holladay to serve as dean of faculty and academic affairs. This new position placed on Holladay's shoulders the responsibility for academic planning, budget oversight, and faculty development.

Challenged to maintain academic excellence in the face of fiscal constraints, LaGree and Holladay began quickly to create formal mechanisms for long-range academic and fiscal planning. If anyone was concerned about whether Candler could keep up the academic pace, that concern was partly laid to rest with the hiring of Luke Timothy Johnson as the first full-time Robert W. Woodruff Professor at Candler.

*In 1992 Luke Timothy Johnson accepted appointment as Candler's first Robert W. Woodruff Professor, the university's most distinguished endowed chair.*

(Jürgen Moltmann and José Miguez Bonino had served previously as Visiting Woodruff Professors.) Candler also secured, with the help of President Laney, its first Nobel Laureate on the faculty, when Archbishop Desmond Tutu served a year as Visiting Woodruff Professor in 1991–92; he would later return in 1998–2000.

Similarly, in student recruitment the school continued its success in competing with the best seminaries and divinity schools in the country. For the fall of 1992 Candler succeeded in luring eighteen of the twenty finalists offered full-ride Woodruff Fellowships, and altogether fifty of the applicants for the fellowships that year ended up enrolling in the fall.

Still, LaGree had plenty of reason for worry. The cumulative effects of low enrollment and high attrition in the previous several years had been masked in part by high enrollment in the MTS program. But the MDiv program was the school's bread and butter. With fluctuating enrollment in seminaries around the country—higher in many conservative seminaries, down in the more mainline schools—LaGree led the faculty in addressing two determinative issues: (1) the size of the student body that Candler could count on year by year, and (2) the size of the faculty and staff that tuition income could support until the endowment grew sufficiently to take pressure off tuition.

At the time, each entering class averaged about 150 MDiv students, 22 MTS students, 10 ThM students, and 19 DMin or STD students. The student-faculty ratio was 10:1, stretching the faculty's capacity. What particularly extended their time and energy was the very work that had helped Candler rise to the top tier of theology schools—the role of Candler as the principal supplier of faculty power to the top-ranked Graduate Division of Religion. While the Department of Religion in Emory College continued to partner with Candler in these programs, throughout the 1990s the Candler faculty contributed 90 to 95 percent of the teaching and advising to PhD students while comprising only 75 percent of the GDR-affiliated faculty.

Enrollment pressures and faculty needs created critical moments of decision about the school's future. In April 1993 the faculty debated raising the minimum grade-point average for admission from 2.25 to 2.75. Those in favor of the change noted that making public a relatively low minimum GPA of 2.25 seemed to lead many outstanding potential applicants to view Candler as not academically challenging. On the other hand, the faculty also recognized that second-career students sometimes have experience, maturity, and intelligence beyond whatever their GPA may have been a decade or more ago, and the school also had the challenge of balancing the church's needs for educated clergy against the faculty preference for high-flying graduate

students. (The story is told of one senior faculty member who, in an orientation session for new PhD students, heard one of them say she hoped one day to teach at the graduate level; he retorted that he hoped to do that himself one day.)

In the end, the faculty raised the bar. Despite the higher GPA requirement, the entering class for the fall of 1994 was the largest in six years. Full-time enrollment continued to hold steady, even as the percentage of applications accepted fell from nearly 90 percent in the fall of 1991 to 74.1 percent in the fall of 1999, when Candler received a record six hundred applications.

In other ways, a more robust admissions program began not only to keep enrollment high but also to change the face of the student body, quite literally. By 1999, international students accounted for fully 9 percent of the Candler enrollment, leading the rest of the university in this growing area of cultivation. Many of these international students hailed from South Korea, with whom Emory and Candler had a historic relationship. (The first international graduate from Emory, in 1893, was a Korean Methodist, Yun Chi-ho. Former Candler dean Jim Laney concluded his Emory presidency when he accepted appointment as U.S. ambassador to Korea in 1993.) Some seventeen countries around the world were represented in the Candler student body in 1999.

Candler also flourished on the development front. In 1990 Emory had launched a five-year campaign to raise $400 million (in the end raising $420 million), of which the goal for Candler was set at $28.5 million. Within two years the school was more than halfway there, having raised $16 million. In LaGree's second year the development staff raised six hundred thousand dollars more than it had raised the previous year.

The endowment grew. In 1991 the endowment designated for Candler amounted to $23 million; five years later it surpassed $100 million, owing largely to bequests from longtime supporters of the school who had been cultivated earlier—Frank and Helen Sherman (Florida Methodists), Sims Garrett (33C), and Bishop William Cannon, whose estate surpassed $11 million. Two years later, the death of Margaret Adger Pitts augmented the endowment still further. To be fair, while most of the cultivation of these friendships had preceded LaGree, he bore the burden of fending off what amounted to creedal tests for the Sherman scholarships and of explaining to aesthetically offended campus constituencies why a bronze eagle was installed on Rudolph Courtyard to honor Sims Garrett.

Meanwhile, the culture wars that roiled American society in the 1980s and 1990s came to Candler. As early as the fall of 1992, LaGree reported in a faculty meeting

**YOUTH THEOLOGICAL INITIATIVE** As mainline denominations and seminaries began to grow increasingly concerned in the 1980s about the pipeline leading through college and seminary to ministry—to be more specific, they were concerned about the diminishing flow through that pipeline—Craig Dykstra, a senior program officer at the Lilly Endowment and a Christian ethicist, conceived of a program to introduce high school students to the prospect of a career in ministry. Launched in 1993 with a grant from Lilly, the Youth Theological Initiative began bringing high school juniors and seniors to Candler every summer. Ecumenical in outreach and outlook, the program helps young people explore their faith in terms of social justice and personal transformation, while engaging in service projects throughout Atlanta. Reflecting on their experience under the guidance of theology faculty in small groups, the students learn to ask questions about God's activity in the world and God's calling upon their own activity—perhaps including careers in ministry.

Since 1999 the YTI has expanded its mission to include offering workshops for local faith communities who want to engage their own young people in similar forms of reflection and service. In the words of its website, YTI "strives to equip young women and men to engage in theological reflection and action, and to ignite their vocational imaginations for the benefit of church and society."

that students had reacted with hostility in the Candler student newsletter, the *Candler Exchange*, to the visit of Carter Heyward to Cannon Chapel. (In the 1970s Heyward had been among the first women ordained to the priesthood in the Episcopal Church.) He also noted student expressions of opposition to homosexuality and to the possible ordination of homosexuals. He told the faculty that in responding to the students, he would stress that the school insisted on the importance of dialogue, even around matters that some considered settled, and he observed that university policy prohibited intimidation of speakers like Heyward; the Emory Police Department, he noted, would be available to enforce this policy. The faculty exhorted him to deal with the substance of these issues as well as with the processes for managing them. In fact, however, process effectively became the constructive means by which to deal with the substance, as the years from 1992 to 1997 would demonstrate.

*Susan Henry-Crowe 76T, recognized as a "maker of Emory history" at the university's 175th anniversary convocation in 2011, served as dean of the chapel and religious life at Emory and played a key role in conversations between the church and the university in managing same-sex commitment ceremonies in university chapels. See Appendix for a biographical sketch.*

Twice during LaGree's deanship the question of homosexuality in the church became an issue threatening to drive a wedge between parts of The United Methodist Church and Emory University. In the first instance, the creation of a university office of lesbian/gay/bisexual student life in 1992 (followed immediately the next year by protection of "sexual orientation" in the Emory nondiscrimination policy) raised consternation among many United Methodists. In 1994 the university took the further step of extending benefits to same-sex domestic partners of employees, equivalent to the kind of benefits available to spouses of employees. (As a concession to church concerns, the university did not extend benefits to opposite-sex domestic partners, because marriage was an option for them in a way that it was not for same-sex partners at the time.)

For some Methodists, these measures looked like a violation of the policy in the *Book of Discipline* that prohibited "advocacy" of homosexuality. Both the dean and the faculty expressed support for the civil rights of homosexual persons, but it appeared

that the school of theology might bear the brunt of ire—and the consequent diminished philanthropy—that followed these decisions of the university administration.

In 1997 the Southeastern Jurisdiction of The United Methodist Church was further riled by the decision of the university to permit same-sex commitment ceremonies in university chapels. The university dean of the chapel took pains to establish guidelines ensuring that such ceremonies would be performed only by clergy whose denominations permitted them. The Emory administration argued that as an extremely diverse community, whose members claimed many different faiths or none, the university could not discriminate against its own community members on the basis of religion. If their religious organizations permitted such ceremonies, they were entitled as Emory community members to use university facilities under certain conditions. Many church members—not just Methodists—objected to what they viewed as Emory supporting the "homosexual agenda," and they raised questions about what it meant for the university to "belong to the Methodist Church," in the words of the university bylaws.

The last two years of LaGree's administration thus required considerable dexterity on his part and that of the school, as they juggled competing demands of their various constituencies. (At the Southeastern Jurisdictional Conference in 2000, the year after LaGree's departure from Emory, delegates presented motions to censure the university and to call for the firing of the university president, William M. Chace, and the dean of the chapel, Susan Henry-Crowe, a 1976 graduate of Candler. These resolutions were defeated, but further bridge building was required over the next four years.)

For many of the faculty members, these cultural and theological debates provided rich fodder for the teaching and educational experience within the curriculum. Candler had always sought to provide intellectual space for wide-ranging theological perspectives. This encouragement of evangelical, liberal, Wesleyan, Lutheran, Calvinist, and Roman points of view was one way of Candler remaining faithful to John Wesley's own legacy of "unreserved openness in conversation with others." One brilliant example of this openness shines forth from a letter that Professor Hendrikus Boers wrote to Dean LaGree in 1994:

> *I had one of the most satisfying MTS colloquys [sic] last night, the kind of thing I have been idealizing about for the School of Theology as a whole. It just so happened that the two students who made their presentation were both evangelicals . . . an MTS/JD student who was in the Law School last year*

*. . . and a graduate student from Biola. And then there was this marvelous giant of an evangelical, physically and in every other way . . . an exceedingly bright mind, working with Walt Lowe on his thesis. But in the group there was also [name], a Hindu, deeply interest[ed] in the Holocaust, and [name], academically among the very best we have admitted to the program, but with no ecclesial affiliation or deeply committed Christian convictions. What a meeting of minds. Questions were very open. . . . I could not help wishing that we could open such a discussion to the School of Theology as a whole. . . . I would very much like to see the openness which manifested itself in this colloquy to take place in a more general way.*

In addition to the intellectual challenges of the time, the mid-1990s at Candler also brought to light certain practical opportunities and threats on the horizon. In 1995 the National Research Council ranked the Graduate Division of Religion

**REBECCA CHOPP**   Arriving at Candler in 1986, one of a half-dozen women who provided a quick infusion of gender balance to the theology faculty in the space of three years, Rebecca Chopp carried with her degrees from Kansas Wesleyan University, Saint Paul School of Theology, and the University of Chicago Divinity School. The first woman to teach systematic theology at Candler, she was the first in many other matters as well. She was the first woman to serve as dean of the faculty and academic affairs at Candler (1993–97) and the first named to a chaired professorship (as Charles Howard Candler Professor of Theology). While chairing the university-wide Commission on Teaching in 1996–97, she demonstrated capacities that made the central administration jealous of the theology school. When the beloved provost of Emory, Billy Frye, stepped down in 1997, President William Chace named Chopp as interim provost and executive vice president for academic affairs, and following a national search she was appointed to the position full-time in 1998. Three years later she left Emory for Yale Divinity School as dean—a step down in the eyes of most—but soon found her footing again as president of Colgate University and, later, Swarthmore College.

at Emory as the fifth-best doctoral program in religion in the United States; this ranking was owing largely to the strength of the Candler faculty, who directed some 90 percent of GDR dissertations. With strong programs in Episcopal studies and Baptist studies, Candler had expanded its ecumenical appeal. Moreover, the possibility of strengthening relationships between the school and The United Methodist Church was aided by the fact that one-third of all United Methodists in the United States lived within four hours of Candler. A younger faculty could look forward to a long, bright future.

On the other hand, the school's facilities needed attention: window panes occasionally fell out of Bishops Hall, and some students had to sit on the floors of overcrowded lecture halls. Architecture was shaping pedagogy, and not in a good way. New seminaries in the region also posed a threat to enrollment; Beeson Divinity School (named for an Emory College graduate, no less—Ralph Waldo Beeson) began

*Jürgen Moltmann, shown here with University Distinguished Professor Jimmy Carter, brought his "theology of hope" to Candler as Visiting Woodruff Professor in the 1980s.*

life three hours away at the Baptist-affiliated Samford University, in Birmingham, Alabama, in 1988, with an endowment of $70 million. Mercer University and New Orleans Baptist Seminary both planted campuses in Decatur, just miles from Emory. For the more evangelically minded, Asbury Seminary in Wilmore, Kentucky, had grown stronger, and Gordon-Conwell Theological Seminary founded a campus in Charlotte, North Carolina, in 1992. Transformations of the old-line denominations threatened the collapse of their structures, and in particular threatened the erosion of the annual contributions of some $1.4 million to Candler through the Ministerial Education Fund of The United Methodist Church.

Balancing these opportunities and challenges, the school looked hard at its institutional effectiveness. Thus, when LaGree announced in the spring of 1999 that he would be leaving to become president of Simpson College, in Iowa, the school had achieved the stability that the university administration had charged him to help establish. Student enrollment had been reduced deliberately because of the constraints presented by facilities, and consequently student quality and the student/faculty ratio had improved. The endowment had been significantly expanded; greater resources thus were available to support teaching and research of the faculty and scholarships for students. Fund-raising annually approached $9 million. The administrative organization had matured enough to give the school structural strength while

*Arthur Keys 92T, recognized as a "maker of Emory history" at the university's 175th anniversary convocation in 2011, found his ministry in leading the largest international relief agency in the world. See Appendix for a biographical sketch.*

remaining relatively lean compared to other schools at Emory. Moreover, Candler had worked hard to keep pace with technological developments (voice mail, email, Ethernet, and full-time information technology staff) and was preparing to plan for new facilities.

LaGree and the faculty had largely met the aims they had identified as priorities early on—strengthening enrollment, building endowment, and increasing engagement with the church. To those three e's, LaGree had added a fourth—the excellence of the faculty—and with the help of strong associate deans and senior leadership he had built on the faculty's international renown.

As a community, the faculty and students had worked hard to maintain their commitment to diversity in all ways, from race and ethnicity to gender and theological perspectives. Candler had attended to its substance and nature as a theologically thoughtful and ecclesially formed body of scholars who are also (and often primarily) people of faith. The school had strengthened the Black Church Studies Program and the Program for Women in Theology and Ministry and had launched a youth initiative. Candler had engaged with its home city through the Atlanta Project and the Faith and the City enterprise. Moreover, the school had helped build an initiative to increase Hispanic enrollment in theology schools and doctoral programs. The year after LaGree's departure, Candler enrolled one hundred African American students for the first time, with a solid international enrollment and growing Latino/Latina presence. True, there remained a strain in the relationship between the church and the university—and thus between the church and Candler. But there also had grown up a more vibrant collaborative effort among alumni and church leaders interested in helping the school.

In the summer of 1999 the university administration turned to Charles "Chuck" Foster to serve Candler as interim dean. The appointment of a search committee ushered in a period of renewed discernment for the faculty to assess what the school most needed in a new dean. High on the list of the faculty's own strengths were its commitment to excellent teaching through pedagogical reflection, peer review, collaborative discussions, and mentoring of pretenure faculty. The faculty also saw opportunity in the vitality of United Methodist churches in the Southeast, and opportunity as well in the changing patterns of ordination and leadership in the mainline denominations, which were opening new conversations about the audience for and the delivery of theological education.

*Dean Russ Richey preaches in Cannon Chapel.*

## CHAPTER TEN

# RENEWING, RECLAIMING, RESTORING

WITH the world about to turn the calendar to a new millennium, the Candler School of Theology was showing signs of age and diminished strength by the year 2000. Yes, the faculty was as robust and productive as ever, and the quality and size of the student body remained healthy. In other dimensions of its life, however, the school faced significant challenges.

The physical facilities of the school had long passed their prime. The old Theology Building, housing Pitts Theology Library, was cramped, ill-lit, and made for an era when technology was no more complicated than a typewriter and a telephone. Bishops Hall, nearly half a century old, offered difficult access for the disabled, and its worn interior resembled nothing so much as a wing of a decaying urban high school. Cannon Chapel had served twenty hard years as one of the busiest buildings on campus and was beginning to need refurbishing.

Worse, the school had lost some goodwill with the church and some relevance to the university. The elevation of a Methodist clergyman to the presidency of Emory in 1977 may have tempted both the university and the church to assume that their relationship would remain strong with hardly any deliberate care and nurturing. But that relationship was strained—ironically and disappointingly— when President James Laney in 1988 charged the Committee on the Church's

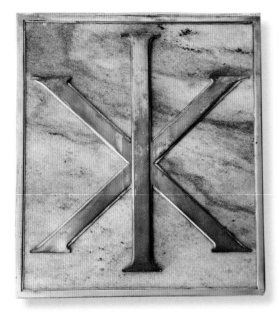

One of the marble symbols originally placed in Durham Chapel and later removed for the renovation of Pitts Theology Library in 1976, this symbol for the Greek Iesous Christos now hangs on the fourth floor of the Rita Anne Rollins Building with its companions.

Presence at Emory University to look closely at the relationship and offer constructive advice for strengthening it. Chaired by Dean Jim Waits, the committee included representatives of the church as well as the university. Over the course of more than a year, the committee considered the fruitful ministries that might arise out of a closer working collaboration among Candler, Glenn Memorial, and the university chaplaincy. In its report, dated February 1989, the committee outlined a series of recommendations, including the hope that the pulpit of Glenn Memorial might be filled through a national search for an eminent preacher, who could build a bridge between church and university by having a faculty role at Candler. (Though the report did not give examples, names mentioned in conversations included William Sloane Coffin Jr. and James Forbes Jr., theological leaders at Yale and Union Seminary, respectively, and later at different times senior pastors at Riverside Church in New York City—not to mention well-known public theologians on matters of war, peace, public health, and restorative justice.) The peremptory rejection of this hope—indeed, the refusal even to entertain the notion—by the conservative North Georgia bishop Ernest Fitzgerald (an Emory trustee), created a strain that never healed during the remainder of Laney's administration.

Several years later, in 1994, the university board appointed a new president, whose quiet agnosticism, while not antagonistic to the church, made it difficult, if not impossible, for him personally to shore up the relationship between Emory and the Southeastern Jurisdiction of United Methodism. William M. Chace came to Emory as its eighteenth president after serving six years as president of another historically (but no longer) Methodist-related institution, Wesleyan University. As he recounted the presidential search in his memoir, *100 Semesters*, "The process sidestepped a potentially difficult issue: religion. . . . Had the search committee asked me if, in fact, I believed in God or had ever had a defining religious moment, I would have been compelled to say No. As an agnostic, I simply have seen no evidence of the existence of God. But . . . that delicate matter never arose."

Among the issues awaiting Chace's resolution when he arrived in Druid Hills was the demand that the university offer benefits to same-sex domestic partners of employees, comparable to benefits for spouses of employees. That issue was soon resolved affirmatively, but not without raising eyebrows in some church quarters.

Further unrest in the Southeastern Jurisdiction was caused in 1997 by the decision of the university to permit same-sex commitment ceremonies in university chapels (see previous chapter). This step led some Methodists in Alabama to call for the church to sever its ties to Emory, much as the church had done when Vanderbilt strayed in 1914. These unhappy Methodists—few but quite vocal—took the Emory bylaws literally and suggested that if Emory actually "belonged to" The United Methodist Church, the church should just go ahead and sell it. Some at Emory tried to imagine a RE/MAX sign at the front gate with a sale price of $11 billion.

To his credit, Dean LaGree had applied his legal mind and his personal suasion to help the university and Candler walk the very fine line between those who passionately wanted progressivism in the church and those who just as passionately wanted orthodoxy at Emory. To their credit, voices on both sides of the issue at Candler expressed as much concern about the health of their community as they did about the theological matters over which they disagreed. But the contest within the larger church was fraught. At the jurisdictional conference in 2000, a year after LaGree's departure, delegates presented motions to censure the university and to call for the firing of the university president and the dean of the chapel, Susan Henry-Crowe. These resolutions were defeated, but tension remained as Candler prepared to welcome a new dean in the fall of that year.

That dean, recruited from Duke Divinity School, was Russell E. Richey. A cradle Methodist, Richey had made his way from his boyhood home of North Carolina to Wesleyan University as an undergraduate, then gradually returned back south, with stops at Union Theological Seminary (in New York City) for a bachelor of divinity degree and Princeton for a PhD. Taking a faculty position in church history at the theology school and graduate school of Drew University, he rose to the rank of professor while also serving for three years as assistant to then president Paul Hardin (son of the United Methodist bishop Paul Hardin, and later chancellor of the University of North Carolina at Chapel Hill). Recruited to Duke in 1986—where his father had taught as well—Richey served there as professor and associate dean.

Arriving at Candler in the fall of 2000, after a decade of frayed relationships between Emory and the church, Richey set about stitching the relationship back together, with strong help from the Candler faculty and staff. His Methodist bona fides were first-class. They included his authorship of *The Methodist Experience in America*, a standard text for the study of Methodism, and years of service to the General Commission on Archives and History of The United Methodist Church, as well as service on the Board of Ordained Ministry of his annual conference. In many ways he embodied the link between church and university, and he threw himself into the taxing work of attending numberless annual conferences, visiting churches without end, and shoring up relations with alumni/ae.

One result of his labor and that of some of the faculty was that Candler came to be viewed as a more centrist school, blending a progressive outlook and constituency with impressive commitments to the evangelical tradition of Methodism. This was, after all, an accurate picture of the place. From a superficial reading, an outsider might view some of the courses being taught as destructive of tradition and orthodoxy. The 1993–94 course bulletin, for instance, described a course taught by Pamela del Couture, assistant professor of pastoral care, as focusing on "pastoral care and social conflict, congregational care and public health, pastoral care and preaching, *critical theory of the family*, and *the role of women in religious and political movements*" (emphasis added); yet it also concluded the description, "with emphasis on the Wesleyan tradition." On the other hand, a different outside observer might think the school was teaching nothing but tradition and orthodoxy, with standard courses of theology and church history abounding—not recognizing that these were being taught by constructive theologians like Walt Lowe and David Pacini, dialectical thinkers like Ted Runyon and Bill Mallard, and Niebuhrians like Clinton Gardner, Ted Weber, Jon Gunnemann, and Jim Fowler.

There was thus a growing realization of Candler as a community of scholars that maintained constructive tension between progressive and conservative theologies—a "realization" both in the sense of "bringing to fruition" and in the sense of "recognition." The Daniel and Lillian Hankey Chair in World Evangelism, the Mack and Rose Stokes Chair in Theology (an estate bequest whose specifics were negotiated by Richey's successor), and the James and Mary Wesley Scholarship all pointed to this successful balancing of perspectives.

Richey also strengthened work with the World Methodist Evangelism Institute, which was housed at Candler. One of the first major programs at the school during his tenure was a conference on evangelism cosponsored with the institute and with The United Methodist Church Board of Discipleship, the Board of Global Ministries, and the Foundation for Evangelism.

Reaching out to alumni/ae, Richey revived the Candler Alumni Council, and he, along with an engaged faculty, rejuvenated the continuing education programs that provided an important link between the seminary and clergy. New appointments to the staff demonstrated a commitment to growing the presence of men and women at Candler from across the full spectrum of Methodism. Key appointments to the faculty not only strengthened Methodist ties but also added women to the faculty.

In many ways Richey was both professionally and temperamentally well suited to this relationship building. His own scholarship was deeply informed by his strong sense of the connectional nature of Methodism, and his demeanor as a genial and slightly rumpled scholar made him approachable. He also knew not to try too hard to remake the school in his own image. In a self-evaluation five years into his deanship, he wrote that he viewed his leadership role in much the same way that he and his wife, Merle, thought of caring for the old homes they had lived in, refurbished, and renewed during their years of marriage. They did not transform but left the structures in place. They ensured the soundness of the foundation and the roof while touching up interior and exterior details. Such work entails a kind of faithfulness to an original design drawn up by someone else. It means adopting a shared vision that one has inherited and has some freedom to refine, but ultimately must pass along intact to succeeding generations.

This understanding of the stewardship he had been called to at Candler shaped Richey's relationship with the faculty, the university, and the church in ways that strengthened the school. (It drove his desire to create at Candler a preeminent Methodist studies program, reflecting the Candler heritage.) This philosophy was, in a way, a noble view of servant leadership. Ultimately, however, it undermined the confidence of some of the faculty in their dean. He was eminently consultative with the faculty about the plans for their house, in all its many dimensions, as if he were a customer-focused architect for a high-end residential client. (As two faculty members would later put it, appreciatively, Richey tried to lead from within the faculty and to build consensus.) In the end, however, some came to want a Frank Lloyd Wright, who would have the temerity to design and cajole them into building a showcase structure, and who would go to the mat for them against forces that seemed beyond their control, whether those forces entailed a sometimes capricious-seeming university administration or an oppressive economic climate. Ironically, this house metaphor became all too literal as Candler's building needs soon reached a critical pass.

Richey's stewardship of Candler faced immediate fiscal challenges when the stock market plummeted in 2000, just two months before his appointment was announced. After the dot-com stock market bubble of the late 1990s burst in the spring of 2000, endowments around the country lost 10 to 25 percent of their value. From August 1999 to March 2000, the Emory endowment

*The christogram Chi Rho incorporates the first two Greek letters of the word for Christ.*

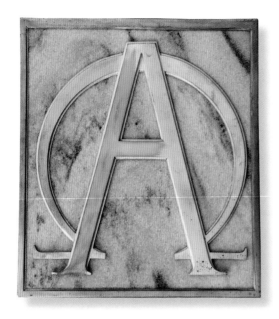

*This Alpha-Omega symbol, which had graced a wall of Durham Chapel, was removed during the 1976 renovation and forgotten in the attic of Bishops Hall until 2012.*

grew by nearly a billion dollars, then lost it all and more over the next eighteen months.

At Candler the impact of the market failure meant that the endowment designated for the school plunged by $50 million over the next three years, from $195 million in 2000 to $171 million in 2001, $157 million in 2002, and $146 million in 2003. (Richey would request an explanation from the administration for this decline, as it appeared that endowments at other schools in the Association of United Methodist Theological Schools were rising during this time; whether he was given that explanation is unclear.) This lost endowment deprived Candler's annual budget of more than $2 million in endowment income (on an annual budget of about $10 million); much of that loss was in scholarship support.

Richey responded to the budget strains by reducing expenditures while trying to keep faculty and staff positions whole. He also began to rebuild the development office, which had been depleted by raids from other institutions. Over the next five years, the thoroughly rebuilt development office succeeded in raising more than $29 million in support of the school of theology. Richey also restructured the administrative offices for greater efficiency and effectiveness. (Steven Kraftchick, who had earned his PhD in New Testament studies from Emory in 1985 and had taught for several years at Princeton before returning to Emory, served with distinction as academic dean until 2003, guiding the school's important reaccreditation. When he stepped out of administration he was replaced by Gail O'Day.)

The fiscal hemorrhaging of Candler was made worse by the anemic condition of the overall Emory budget. The projected commitments of the university to retirement benefits and health-care costs for faculty and staff began to loom increasingly large in the face of new budgetary constraints, especially as health-care costs continued to rise nationally. In his very first meeting with the Candler faculty, in August 2000, Richey reported that the university administration was requiring all schools to reduce their projected expenses for the following budget cycle by 3 percent; for Candler this reduction amounted to almost all of the three hundred thousand dollars that the administration had pledged the previous May to help support student recruitment. In 2001, with little (some would say no) consultation with the deans or faculty, the university administration took the unpopular step of reducing health-care and retirement benefits for faculty and staff as a cost-saving measure. The individual schools and colleges of the university also were required to assume more of the cost of those benefits. Morale suffered.

The gravest impact of the economic downturn was delay in a building project that had long been in the works. As early as the end of Jim Waits's deanship, with the approval and encouragement of the university administration, Candler had begun to plan a new theology school building. While recruiting Richey to the deanship, President Chace and Provost Rebecca Chopp had assured him that the university had an obligation to bring the facilities of Candler up to the standards of those of other Emory schools and colleges. (Bishops Hall was the only building on the Quadrangle or its periphery that had not had extensive renovation within the previous fifteen years.) The university committed to provide a similar level of funding to Candler that it had made in recent years to the schools of nursing, public health, and business. That level had been 50 percent of the cost for brand-new homes for these schools, with the other 50 percent coming from the schools through unrestricted endowment and fundraising.

Plans called for a fifteen-thousand-square-foot addition to Pitts Library; renovation of Bishops Hall; and construction of a new, thirty-five-thousand-square-foot building north of Bishops, for a combined total cost of $32 million. Candler would be responsible for half: $16 million. The school thus would have three buildings—its original 1916 home, the half-century-old Bishops, and a brand-new facility. In addition, Cannon Chapel would continue to serve both Candler and the larger university through coordinated scheduling. During the whole of Richey's deanship, the status of this building project created anxiety and uncertainty among the faculty about the place of Candler on the list of Emory's priorities, and indeed among the nine planets of Emory's intellectual solar system—its schools and colleges.

By 2003 the university administration had cut the capital match program from 50 percent to 25 percent; Candler argued that whatever the eventual building project would look like or cost, the university had made a commitment of $16 million. At one point it appeared that donors for new buildings in the School of Medicine and the Goizueta Business School had already made funds available while Candler was still raising money, and the theology school fought to hold its place as first in line for new construction. One way to effect this placeholding would be to form an alliance with another potential building tenant that could bring some money to the project; this partner turned out to be the Center for Ethics, which had garnered a lead gift. (That gift, unfortunately, would not materialize, owing to a crash in the housing market and the donor's fortune.) Meanwhile, each year of delay added $1.5 million to projected costs.

At one point the interim provost (following Chopp's departure for Yale Divinity School), Howard "Woody" Hunter, proposed moving the entire theology school to the site of the former Protestant Radio and Television Center (now Emory Point) on Clifton Road. In many ways such a move would have served Candler well. The move would have allowed development of something that Candler had never really had in the entirety of its history—a residential theology school community, where the formation of people for ministry could occur effectively amid a residential campus as well as in the classroom and chapel. Moreover, as the proposal was presented by Hunter, the university would have borne more of the cost of construction in exchange for recouping the Theology Building on the Quadrangle and Bishops Hall.

But the prospect of relocating Candler more than a mile away, at the edge of campus farthest from the academic center of the university, caused deep consternation and alarm among many of Candler's faculty members, who rejected the concept. In their view the move would represent in physical terms the intellectual marginalization of religion and theology in the modern university. For a faculty that valued ideas as much as the practical aspects of professional formation, such a proposal was unacceptable. (On the other hand, and ironically, the presence of the school at that spot on Clifton Road would have made it the principal gateway into the university from the northwest. As it is, that gateway is now a mixed-use block of four-story retail and apartment buildings, the kind found in any upscale developing area.)

At last, by May 2005, it appeared that ground-breaking could take place the following year, but Emory's provost at the time, Earl Lewis, met with the Candler faculty in October 2005 to offer a whole new concept. Instead of the renovation of Pitts Library and Bishops Hall and construction of a third building, Candler could have two new buildings to replace Bishops Hall and the 1916 Theology Building (which housed Pitts Library). Bishops would be razed, and the Theology Building on the Quadrangle would be restored to its pre-1976 appearance and rededicated for use by Emory College of Arts and Sciences. The college would move several departments or programs into the Quadrangle building, which would have public spaces available for use by the university community, including Candler. Assuming that the college departments might be religion, Middle Eastern studies, and Jewish studies, the building would retain some of its original thematic purpose of instruction in religion. (In the end, the old Quadrangle building proved too costly for the college, but the theology school went ahead with the concept anyway, and the university assumed the cost of renovating the 1916 structure.)

The university administration pitched the concept as a strategic investment to maintain Candler as the preeminent theology school in the country. Two modern buildings could be operated more efficiently than one new building and two old ones, thus saving the school significant operating expenses in the long run. In the end the university also committed to a 40 percent match on both of the new buildings—to the tune of $23.4 million of the final $58.5 million total.

Meanwhile the Candler faculty regrouped and prepared to make Bishops Hall livable for the interim.

*The circle around the simple Greek cross represents eternity.*

Despite these demoralizing setbacks, the Candler faculty and administration were reaping the fruits of innovative and important developmental work. The Lilly Endowment granted a continuation of its support for the Youth Theological Initiative. The Alonzo McDonald Family Chair in Jesus and Culture, a gift of Emory College alumnus and former Emory trustee Alonzo McDonald 48C, brought to Candler such visiting luminaries as Jaroslav Pelikan in 2001, John T. Noonan Jr. in 2002, Alice Parker in 2003, and Wayne A. Meeks in 2004. (Later visitors have included Herbert Kessler, Randall Balmer, David Steinmetz, Thomas Lynch, Barbara Brown Taylor, James Carroll, and the dean of the faculty of theology at Africa University, Beauty Maenzanise. Not to be confused with this chair, a different Alonzo McDonald chair was conferred in 2005 on John Witte, director of the Center for the Study of Law and Religion, in the Emory School of Law.)

Perhaps of greatest significance for the long-term health of both the church and the university writ large was a Lilly Endowment grant of $10 million in 2002 to support a new multidisciplinary program in practical theology and religious practice. Intended to produce forty new doctors of philosophy for the next generation of teaching in theology schools, the program encompassed the study of worship, preaching, teaching, social justice, and congregational leadership while enhancing the collaboration of Candler with the Graduate Division of Religion in the disciplines of ethics, Hebrew Bible, historical studies, and West and South Asian religions. This grant provided public ratification of the degree to which the faculty of the school had established itself as a major contributor—perhaps the primary contributor—to the professoriate in theological disciplines.

In spite of budget woes, building obstacles, and a growing sense of national unease brought on by the events of September 11, 2001, the vitality of the school of theology never seemed to wane during the first years of the twenty-first century. Applications for admission to all degree programs reached their highest level in a decade, and in some years the school exceeded its budgeted enrollment, so that additional tuition monies could fill in some of the budget gaps.

Keeping the faculty whole against the depredations of other schools proved a more daunting challenge. In addition to losing one friend and colleague (William Lawrence) to the deanship of Perkins, Richey lost another (Stephen Gunter) to the presidency of Young Harris College. More than a dozen other faculty members or administrators heard siren songs from Yale, Duke, Harvard, and elsewhere but mostly resisted. Almost always Richey persuaded his colleagues to stay—perhaps because in most instances the grass was not much greener elsewhere.

The school also shored up its commitments to ecumenical partnerships. Richey early on had demonstrated a personal openness to understanding and dialogue with traditions other than Methodism: his dissertation at Princeton had been about English Unitarianism. During his deanship the faculty sharpened and strengthened the work of other traditions at Candler, even while building up the connections between Candler and The United Methodist Church. The programs in Baptist studies and Anglican studies (the "mother church" of Methodism, after all) gained focus and energy. At the same time, the work of the Aquinas Center at Emory became clearer under the guidance of Dana Greene (formerly dean of Oxford College of Emory University), and the ties of Candler and Emory to the Roman Catholic community were thereby strengthened. Richey also worked deliberately and tirelessly to try to make Candler the North American center of Wesleyan studies, but that aim was thwarted in part by a few scholars' refusal to be recruited away from their devotion to Duke basketball, and the departure of another for the Perkins deanship. All of this required some delicate balancing of competing interests. As he would remark near the end of his deanship, those who would like Candler to be more Methodist had their counterparts in those who would like it to be less so.

In the context of graduate study of religion, these years brought good balance between the Candler School of Theology, with its focus on Christianity and theology, and the Department of Religion in Emory College, where the study of world religions and cultural phenomena predominated. Under the guidance of members of the theology faculty during this time—especially Elizabeth Bounds, Jon Gunnemann, Carl

Holladay, and Steve Tipton, who all served terms one after the other in codirecting the Graduate Division of Religion—the graduate study of religion at Emory continued to flourish by means of remarkable collaboration.

In the fall of 2003 a new university administration started with the advent of James W. Wagner as president. Wagner quickly set in motion a process that would lead to the unveiling of a university-wide strategic plan in 2005. As part of that process, Candler engaged with every other division of the university and found congenial conversation partners in sometimes surprising places (physics and neurosciences, for example) and other times familiar places (studies in race and difference, or programs in ethics and law). Soon the theme of "religions and the human spirit" emerged as one of the focal points for development in the new strategic plan. Once the "queen of the sciences" in the medieval university, theology had gradually been shunted aside in favor of other disciplines and professions. Yet now theology found common cause with schools of nursing and public health, with which it created a certificate in religion and health. Candler strengthened existing cross-disciplinary programs with the schools of law and business. It explored issues of religion and violence with the Carter Center. It soon moved into the same building as the Emory Center for Ethics. In short order the Candler School of Theology had been restored to a more central position within the university—not only physically but intellectually.

One initiative that Richey proposed in response to the announcement of the university Strategic Initiatives Fund to jump-start vitality in the schools was a request for five hundred thousand dollars to renovate Turner Village as well as funds for faculty chairs and student scholarships. Michael Mandl, the executive vice president for finance and administration at Emory, suggested that Candler focus on the chairs and scholarships—leading Richey to infer (correctly, as it turned out) that the university had its collective eye on Turner Village, which would become Emory Point.

Nevertheless, as the strategic plan started and plans for the new building were drawn up, Richey found himself much like Moses—unable, in the end, to enter the promised place of flourishing and new life. After five years of difficult circumstances, a number of Candler's faculty members began to bruit about the notion that a change of leadership would be necessary to achieve the vision offered by the strategic plan and the prospect of a new building. At the end of 2005, Richey announced that he would step down after serving one more year, while the university undertook a search for his successor.

*Candler occupied the Rita Anne Rollins Building in 2008.*

## CHAPTER ELEVEN

# POTENTIAL CATASTROPHES, CREATIVE RESPONSE

WHEN the search for Russ Richey's successor started in August 2005—with a committee chaired by Emory College dean Robert Paul and populated by Candler faculty, staff, students, and alumni (as well two Emory trustees, one of whom was a bishop and alumnus)—the challenge was steep.

Determined to maintain the identity of Candler as a United Methodist seminary in every way possible, the committee promulgated a search that underscored the need for the dean to have the right denominational affiliation—United Methodist. Yet, as the previous two deans' searches at Candler had demonstrated, it was difficult enough finding a highly regarded academic who wanted the increasingly onerous and fund-raising–centered work of dean. The task was made harder by limiting the pool to candidates from a single denomination. Out of 8 million United Methodists in the United States, could the committee find one person suitable for the job?

In the end, of course, the committee did. She was working on Riverside Drive, in New York City, as the chief executive of the Women's Division of The United Methodist Church General Board of Global Ministries. Her name was Jan Love, and she stepped into the Candler dean's office on January 1, 2007.

The appointment was unusual, not only because Love was the first woman to lead the school in its ninety-plus years, but also because she was the first dean

with no pastoral experience and, indeed, no seminary degree. She had graduated from Eckerd College before earning master's and PhD degrees in political science at Ohio State University. While she had distinguished herself as a scholar and teacher at the University of South Carolina, her field was international relations, where she focused on the nexus of politics and religion. One indication of her capacity to think creatively in terms of religion on a world stage was that, while she began her career at South Carolina in government and international studies, her last three years at the university included an appointment as associate professor in the Department of Religious Studies.

Although some constituents of Candler expressed reservations about naming a seminary leader who lacked a seminary degree, Love knew the church well. As the daughter of a United Methodist minister (James N. Love 56T), she had gained intimate experience of life in the parish. As a high school student in the Alabama–West Florida Conference in the 1970s, she had been nominated to serve on the UMC Board of Global Missions. As a college student, she had attended the 1975 World Council of Churches meeting in Nairobi, Kenya, where her fellow delegates elected her—a youngster among them—to the WCC central committee, on which she served for the next twenty-three years.

Bishop Marshall "Jack" Meadors 58T, who was bishop-in-residence at Candler when Love was named dean—and who had known her from his time as a minister in South Carolina before he was elected bishop—called her arrival at Candler "providential and exciting." Noting her commitment to Christ and the church, her scripture-based Wesleyan faith, and her experience in the global multireligious environment, he applauded her "strength of mind, heart, and character to deal with tough issues, and to do it with gentleness, kindness, patience, and a sense of humor."

First on her agenda—after getting to know the faculty and the lay of the land—was coming to terms with a quickly developing future. Under the leadership of a new president, James Wagner, who had arrived in August 2003, Emory University had prepared and launched a strategic plan in the fall of 2005. The plan was intended to map the path for the university over the next decade. Each of the nine colleges and schools at Emory likewise had developed its own strategic goals, so as to harmonize with the larger institutional aims, maximize possible collaborations and synergy, and attend simultaneously to its more parochial needs and ambitions.

For Candler, those goals did not differ significantly from what they had been in the previous three decades: building faculty distinction, creating an educationally rich experience for students, addressing the impact of new technology on pedagogy, achieving international eminence, forging closer alliances with the church writ large, and doing so with fiscal soundness in decent facilities.

Regarding the student experience, the faculty had undertaken a revision of the curriculum in 2004 and was preparing to roll out the new program. The fall of 2007 ushered in the full scope of changes that the faculty had voted to implement: a required core of study instead of discipline-based distribution requirements; a revised contextual education experience to integrate the place of ministry and coursework more closely; new interdisciplinary concentrations that encouraged students to change their learning and competencies across the curriculum; a system of advising that ushered students more quickly and seamlessly into academic life at Candler and the university; and a requirement that every student take at least one course in a religion other than Christianity, in recognition of the increasingly global and interreligious context of ministry.

The imperative of maintaining faculty distinction pressed hard on the dean and the faculty. The previous decades had seen the appointment of faculty members

*In 2006 Jan Love was named dean of Candler—the first woman to hold the position.*

whose work in many ways defined their respective fields: Brooks Holifield, Don Saliers, Roberta Bondi, James Fowler, Jon Gunnemann, Fred Craddock. One by one these leaders in the field of theological education began to retire or anticipate retirement. Others, somewhat younger but equally influential—Steve Tipton, Luke Johnson, Tom Long—could be seen following close behind them. A generational transition in the faculty meant the need for serious thought about wooing the next raft of star faculty members.

During that first year of Love's deanship, Candler also witnessed the breaking of ground for the first phase of a mammoth construction project, as the school began work on its new classroom and office building. In August 2008 the school occupied this building, now called the Rita Anne Rollins Building, which Candler shares with the Emory Center for Ethics. Immediately preparations began for Phase II, intended to house the Pitts Theology Library as well as a new teaching chapel and public spaces for community formation. These two buildings would double the physical space for Candler but also would increase substantially the recurring costs for maintenance and operations.

As always, the challenges around recruitment and admission of students raised both concerns and hopes for the school. At the end of her first year Dean Love noted that, while the number of Methodist students at Candler had increased, they remained slightly less than a majority of the student body; since that percentage affected the

*Phase II of the Candler building project, shown here in an architect's rendering, was scheduled to open in 2014.*

flow of scholarship support from the Ministerial Education Fund of The United Methodist Church, the school would do well to have still more Methodist students. On a more positive note, the percentage of students from the southeastern United States had declined to 80 percent from 88 percent the previous year, indicating a continuing national expansion of the recruitment base and a further step toward the goal of establishing Candler as the top-ranked theology school in the country. These two trends, however, pointed to the need for astute and continual balancing of goals: national eminence and regional influence.

Over the next five years the school joined the rest of the university in tracking the path toward certain strategic goals. Candler kept a scorecard in those areas. Aiming to have "a world-class, diverse faculty," Candler aimed to have 30 percent of its teaching and research faculty receive external research funding. In fact that percentage fluctuated from a low of 8 percent in 2012 to a high of 75 percent in 2008, the last an anomalous outlier well beyond the typical 20 to 25 percent during this period. Intending for its faculty to be recognized for leadership in their various fields, the school set a target of 85 percent of faculty to serve in "formal leadership positions" in their fields (for instance, the presidency of a learned society or editorship of a major journal); that number ranged from 60 percent in 2009 to as high as 71 percent in 2012. Most remarkably, in 2009–10 alone, fully one-third of all the books published by Emory University faculty were published by Candler faculty members.

Arguably these somewhat arbitrary targets serve merely to diagnose symptoms of greatness—the pulse and vital signs of excellence, as it were. They did not fully measure the passion of teaching, the skill of mentoring, the scholarly insight, the spark of creativity in the classroom that are the substance of an eminent faculty. But they pointed in the right direction.

Just as telling about the quality of the educational experience at Candler were the trends in student enrollment during this period. As the university set the strategic goal of enrolling "the best and brightest . . . students" and providing "exemplary support for them to achieve success," Candler sought to enhance or maintain the diversity of its student body. With a target of 50/50 enrollment of women and men, the school held steadily at 49 to 53 percent female enrollment between 2009 and 2012. Striving to attract 10 percent of its students from abroad, Candler variously dipped to 8 percent and rose to 13 percent during this time. Aiming for 30 percent U.S. ethnic minority enrollment by 2015, Candler reached this mark by 2010 and increased the number to 38 percent in 2012–13.

Significantly, by 2008–9 Candler also had the largest tenured or tenure-track

African American faculty of any seminary in the country. That year the school launched the Erskine-Smith-Moseley Fund, a scholarship endowment honoring faculty members Noel Erskine, Luther Smith, and the late Romney Moseley. The school also planned to honor its first African American faculty member, the late Grant Shockley, by naming a seminar room for him in Phase II of its building program. The success of Candler in recruiting minority and female faculty members also made the school vulnerable to raids. During Love's administration Robert Franklin became president at Morehouse College (he would return as the Laney Professor in 2014), Alton Pollard became dean of the Howard University School of Divinity, Mary Elizabeth Moore became dean of the Boston University School of Theology, Gail O'Day became dean of the Wake Forest School of Divinity, and Michael Brown became associate dean of Wabash College. These appointments demonstrated that Candler has been for many years a remarkable proving ground, but they also drained the school of senior female and African American faculty.

In addition to the achievements of the faculty, the quality of the student body continued to rise. By 2012 the percentage of applicants admitted to all programs had dropped to 75.6 percent from 90 percent in previous years, and the percentage of admissions to the MDiv program was 79 percent. The GPA of the entering class continued to inch upward annually, from 3.28 in 2009 to 3.34 in 2012.

Significant challenges loomed for the school, however. One of those was a problem confronting every theological seminary in the country—the increasing number of "nones" (that is, persons in society at large who on surveys indicate "none" as their religious affiliation) and the consequent decline of interest in ministry through the organized church. According to a study released by the Pew Forum on Religion and Public Life in October 2012, the number of American adults who claimed no religious affiliation had risen from 15 percent to nearly 20 percent in the five previous years, and included some 13 million self-identified agnostics and atheists. Most of these adult Americans, according to the Pew report, were not antireligious; they believed that religious organizations and activities actually benefit society. But they were not seeking religious affiliation, and more than a third of them described themselves as "spiritual but not religious"—also known by the acronym SBNR. The ranks of Protestant Christians fell from 53 percent of American adults in 2007 to 48 percent in 2012; both evangelical and mainline white Protestants reported the most significant decline, while black Protestants, Mormons, Roman Catholics, and Orthodox Christians held steady.

*The atrium of Phase II is intended to provide space for community.*

The rise in religiously unaffiliated Americans was particularly visible from generation to generation. That is, moving from the World War II generation through the baby boom to younger millennials (born between 1990 and 1994), the percentage of religiously unaffiliated members rose with each succeeding generation. These data suggested that the coming years would witness a continued decline in religious connection to the church.

*shown here is one of two works by John August Swanson with the same title,* Washing of the Feet.

Moreover, the previous four decades had seen a steady diminution in membership and a rising average age of members in churches; in United Methodism alone, membership dropped from 13 million to 8 million between 1968 and 2007, and in 2007 the average age of members was sixty. Moreover, mainline Protestant churches had begun to experience a growing crisis in leadership. According to one study, only 5 percent of United Methodist Church elders were under the age of thirty-five in 2007, compared to 15 percent in 1985. The median age of United Methodist elders in 2008 was fifty-four—half older, half younger. Thus, the pool of prospective denominational leaders for the decades ahead was shrinking. At the same time, while fewer men and women appeared to be seeking (or staying in) careers in ministry, some mainline churches were beginning to shutter their doors. In 2010 the Presbyterian Church (USA) closed eighty-eight churches, and United Methodist worship attendance dropped annually through 2011.

What all of this shift in church membership and religious affiliation meant for the churches served by Candler—and thus, also, for Candler itself—was a growing strain on mission. To begin addressing some of the concerns raised by these demographic trends, Love created the new position of associate dean of United Methodist studies and filled it with Anne Burkholder 77T 92PhD, who had had extensive experience both in the parish and in conference leadership positions in Florida. Love also built on the outside review of the Office of Church Ministries Education initiated by Dean Richey; on the strength of the recommendations from that review she separated the Methodist Studies Program from the Office of Lifelong Learning and recruited Robert Winstead, a clergy member of the North Georgia Conference, to guide the latter office in working more effectively to offer continuing education programs. Candler also created the new position of pastor-theologian in residence to foster creative conversations between students and experienced church leaders.

Dean Love also began pushing for more scholarship support, particularly to seal the deal with the best applicants. As Vanderbilt Divinity School introduced a merit-based scholarship that was more munificent than the Woodruff Scholarship, Candler found itself losing in head-to-head competition with the Nashville institution. Bishop Candler might be rolling in his grave. By the spring of 2009 a new program called Candler Leadership had turned around this situation, and that year Candler enrolled some three-quarters of its top applicants and lost few, if any, to Harvard, Boston, Duke, Yale, or Vandy.

Fortunately the development office continued to succeed in drawing supporters to the school. Emory launched the public phase of a $1.6 billion fund-raising campaign in September 2008, just as Lehman Brothers was declaring bankruptcy and the world economy was preparing to nosedive into the Great Recession. Despite the challenges that came with what President Wagner described as a "new economic climate," Candler stepped up its activities and its successes. Within two years—and with another two to go in the campaign—Candler had raised $39.8 million, some 58 percent of its campaign goal of $60 million. By the end of the campaign, on December 31, 2012, the school had raised $65.4 million. (Its goal was third-highest among all schools at Emory, behind Emory College and Goizueta Business School, each with many more alumni than Candler had.) At least part of the success was owing to the enlargement of the pool of Candler donors, including a reinvigorated Committee of One Hundred.

All of this development was to the good, and it was essential. The recession of 2008 did what the recession of 2000 had done—sap the Emory endowment of about $1 billion, some 20 percent of its total. To address a shortfall of $15 million in endowment income, the university eliminated subsidies to some schools and reduced the subsidy to Candler by 40 percent—about $1.5 million of the 2009–10 budget and about $2 million of the 2010–11 budget. The school projected budget deficits of $1.2 million in fiscal

year 2011 and $1.7 million in fiscal year 2012, and the college no longer could pony up $7.5 million for the old Theology Building on the Quadrangle. Candler needed every new donor it could find, and Dean Love and the development staff hit the circuits continually to find and introduce themselves to those donors.

Meanwhile, creative developments in the academic programs were under way. To respond to the framing principle of internationalization in the university strategic plan, Candler formed a faculty committee on international studies, and Love appointed a director of international initiatives. The school negotiated an array of memos of understanding with other theology schools and educational institutions, ranging from the Evangelical Seminary of Puerto Rico to St. Paul's (Anglican) University in Kenya, and from Yonsei University in Korea to United Theological College in India. In 2009 a partnership with International Relief and Development (an NGO founded by Candler alumnus Arthur B. Keys Jr.—see chapter 12) enabled six students and four faculty members to participate in internships in the Republic of Georgia, Indonesia, and Mozambique. Closer to home, Candler in 2010–11 ratified a partnership with General Theological Seminary, the Episcopal school in New York City, to transfer some eighty thousand to ninety thousand books to Pitts Library and to initiate exchange programs for students and faculty.

Responding to the deepening complexity (and opportunity) of the digital environment, Candler initiated a partnership with the Sloan Consortium to train three cohorts of faculty over three summers (2011–13) in the use of digital resources for teaching online or hybrid courses; most of these courses were centrally important to the MDiv curriculum. The Sloan initiative was intended to help Candler make judgments about the best use of online courses in the face of burgeoning interest in massive online open courses, or MOOCs.

Simultaneously, Candler sought to bolster traditional offerings, revising the MTS curriculum and proposing a new MA in religious studies. (The MA lacked the support of the James T. Laney School for Graduate Studies, which awards graduate degrees in the arts and sciences at Emory, and so the degree could not be implemented.) More effectively still, Candler dished up a menu of strong entrees for persons seeking professional development. The DMin, phased out more than a decade earlier, was reintroduced in response to strong interest by alumni and church leaders; this time around the degree depended largely on the technology of distance learning. Two new master's degrees—in religious leadership and in religion in public life—met the interest of religious leaders for focused advanced training in leadership. Reaching out to a large potential audience in the Atlanta metropolitan area hungry for lifelong learning, Candler drew on its considerable resources in liturgical studies to offer a certificate program in music and worship, although this program met with less success than consultants had advised it would. All of this activity grew, in part, from the recognition that some 45 percent of the income at Candler derived from tuition, primarily in the MDiv track, and that another 40 percent came from the endowment; with both of these sources at risk in the future, Candler simply needed to find new streams of revenue.

To its great credit, the faculty undertook all of these curricular innovations and refinements while continuing its commitment to the Graduate Division of Religion, which annually enrolled about 150 PhD students and awarded 18 to 25 doctorates a year. Two-thirds of the Candler faculty taught in the program, which accepted less than 7 percent of its nearly three hundred applicants each year.

*Candler houses the largest collection of paintings by John August Swanson. Shown here is The Last Supper.*

Perhaps most creatively, Candler continued to imagine ways to enhance the preparation of students for careers in ministry. In 2008 the Candler Advantage program was launched, offering students an opportunity to spend the summer working full-time in a setting of their choice while earning a stipend of eight thousand dollars—thus gaining valuable experience at the same time they offset the cost of their education. Equally significant, in a period of rising consumer debt throughout America—debt from which clergy are hardly exempt—the school offered a noncredit fall seminar on financial planning and debt management.

One of the legacies of the Love administration will be the founding of the Laney Legacy in Moral Leadership, which honors the enduring contributions of James T.

and Berta R. Laney. Dr. Laney's service as a missionary, educator, and ambassador bore the stamp of someone who understood that true moral leadership expresses the wisdom, hopes, and vision of a community in response to a transcendent good. Mrs. Laney, whose long partnership with her husband complemented his work in countless ways, also forged her own moral leadership through commitments to pastoral care in clinical settings, a ministry of hospitality, and engagement in working for justice and peace. Emory honored both of the Laneys by bestowing honorary degrees on them in 1994. A chaired professorship anchors the Laney Legacy program and makes possible courses in moral leadership. In addition, the Laney Professor guides an advanced summer internship program for second- and third-year Candler students who demonstrate the potential for careers that carry forward the kind of moral leadership that the Laneys modeled.

In terms of the relationship with The United Methodist Church, Love continued to build on the work of Dean Richey. President Wagner provided great support here; his own faith commitments not only made him sympathetic to the complementary missions of church and university but also gave him the language with which to foster communication in both directions. As Candler hosted various gatherings of church officials, ecclesiastical bodies, visiting bishops, and others, Wagner readily complied when called upon to speak to these groups about the heritage and mission of Emory as they continue to resonate with the interests and mission of the church in the twenty-first century.

The school has the advantage of a clear mission statement and a clear set of values. The 2012 self-study of the school articulated those "six core values" in the following way:

- Candler is embedded in the Christian tradition.
- Candler stands for the highest standard of intellectual and theological integrity.
- Candler celebrates the value of diversity.
- Candler has an ecumenical vision of the church.
- Candler is committed to social justice.
- Candler is a community of formative practices.

Summing up the identity, commitments, and culture of the Candler School of Theology, Dean Love remarked,

*This long-standing clarity about basic matters of identity represents this community's strong commitment to professional training for ministry and theological scholarship, which we believe to be complementary and necessary for the excellence of both. Within this integrated vision, deeply held differences are expected—even celebrated—and discussions about them feature grace, dignity, civility, and deep respect for the personhood of the one who holds them. Many other institutions and faculties in higher education and theological education have no common clarity about who they are and where they are going over the long term. Many struggle with factionalism related to religious, theological, doctrinal, ideological, and/or methodological differences. In contrast, the hallmarks of Candler's culture, perhaps beginning with Dean Cannon, are not only clarity of purpose and identity, but also a gracious ecumenical generosity in the community's fundamental understanding that the interplay of genuine differences can strengthen a community.*

As the Candler School of Theology approached 2014, the last years of its first century of existence in some ways reflected the state of the world that had prevailed a hundred years earlier. Major cultural shifts in 1914 marked the end of the Victorian world and the entrance into modernity, just as major cultural shifts in 2013 suggested that the second century at Candler would usher in a new era defined by a different name than "modern" or even "postmodern." New forms of technology gaining popularity and influence in 1914—the telephone, the mass-produced automobile, radio, cinema, air travel—transformed life around the world while delivering to schools of theology new tools, opportunities, and demands. Similarly the swift unfolding of mind-boggling digital technology leading up to the centennial of Candler presented an array of nearly miraculous forms of communication and—to use a good Methodist term—connection. Just as the economic, social, and educational expectations and commitments of the Progressive Era led to new pressures on educational and religious institutions, so the changing national dynamics of immigration, income disparity, and the health of the economy posed serious questions about the priorities and well-being of theology schools and churches. Making the most of these transformations will require the diligent exercise of imagination and creativity.

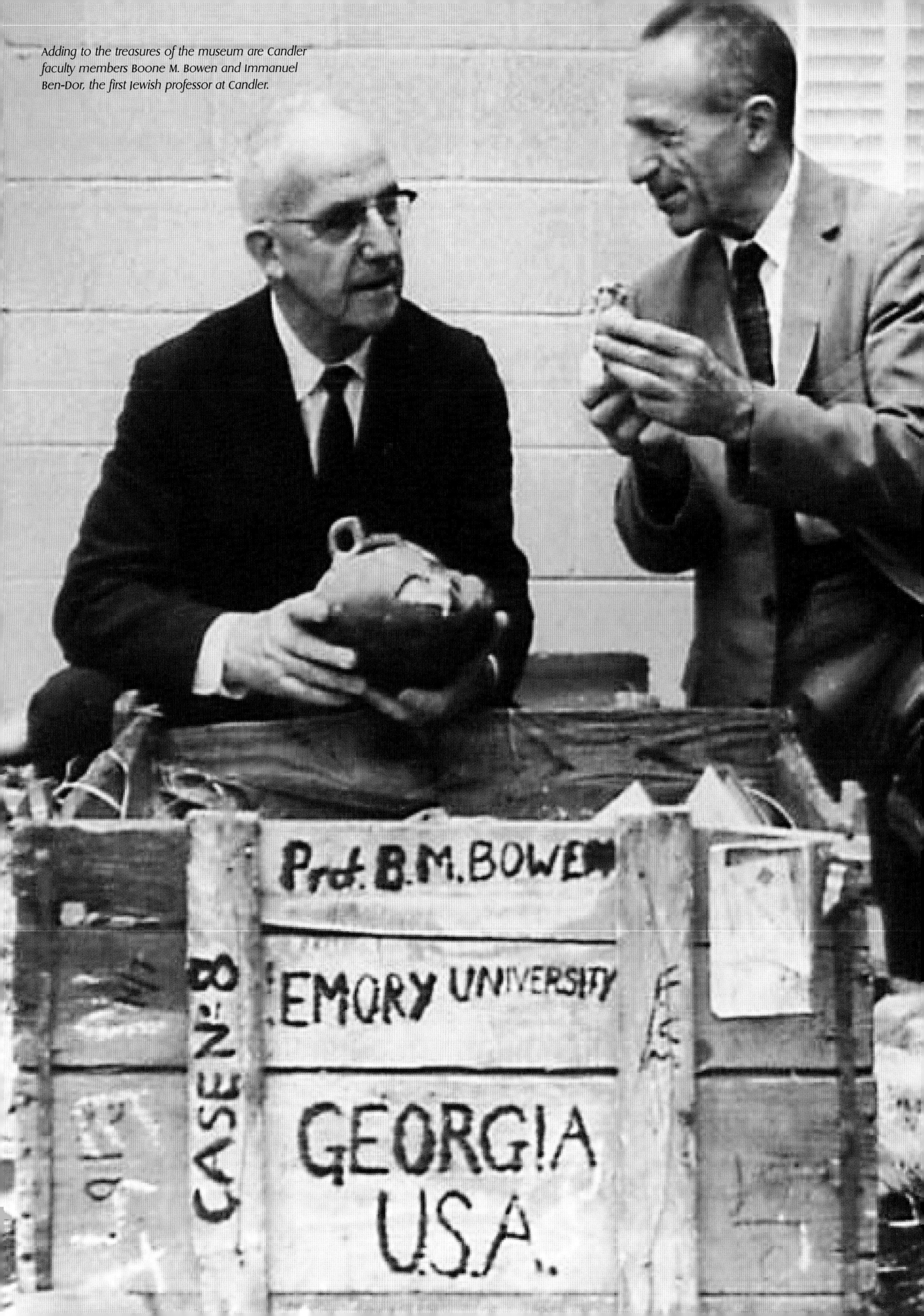

Prof. B.M. BOWE
EMORY UNIVERSITY
CASE No 8
GEORGIA
U.S.A.

*Adding to the treasures of the museum are Candler faculty members Boone M. Bowen and Immanuel Ben-Dor, the first Jewish professor at Candler.*

# A Theology School in the Context of a University

## Candler and Emory, Take One

When a university (in this case, Emory) comprises a number of colleges and schools (in this case, nine), some points of comparison among them are bound to crop up. And just as children in a large family might wonder whether one of them is most favored, so it is with the schools.

At Emory the answer has not always been clear. The Emory College of Arts and Sciences is the firstborn, the largest, the one with the widest acquaintance in the world, and the one with the most complex personality. But the School of Medicine, next oldest, has at least an equal claim to eminence and impact globally, while the other professional schools—and Oxford College, on the founding campus—all just as forthrightly step forward to ask, "What about me? Don't I make a distinctive contribution as well?"

Many creative ways exist to measure the centrality and importance of a school or college to its university. How many graduates does it send forth compared to the other schools of the university? What proportion of the university

endowment does it own and draw upon for income? How does it rank among its national peers, and does that ranking raise or lower the reputation of the university as a whole? When its faculty members give public lectures on campus, who shows up? Do its faculty members hold elected leadership positions in the university, and do they win prestigious university-wide awards for scholarship, teaching, and service? Do its alumni serve the university to an unusual degree?

By any of these measures, the Candler School of Theology can claim to have had a disproportionate impact at Emory based on the size of its faculty and its student body. Since 1915, when Emory University was chartered, 156 alumni have served on the Emory University board of trustees—24 of them with degrees from Candler. This does not include 4 faculty members who served on the board apart from their service on the faculty: Plato Durham before becoming dean, Lavens Thomas after leaving the faculty for the pastorate, and William Cannon and Mack Stokes after their election to the episcopacy. Counting only the graduate and professional schools, the 24 trustees from Candler compare to 33 with degrees from the law school, 21 from business, 14 from medicine, 6 from the graduate school, 2 from dentistry, and 1 from public health. Yet alumni of Candler number fewer than those of all other schools except dentistry, which closed in 1990, and public health, which opened in 1990.

Faculty impact is likewise impressive. Emory bestows the Thomas Jefferson Award at commencement each year in recognition of extraordinary service to the university through personal activities, influence, and leadership. It is the premier honor for a faculty member or senior administrator. First awarded in 1962, it was given in 1989 to William Mallard, professor of church history at Candler, and in 2007 to Melissa Maxcy Wade 72C 76G 96T 00T, director of the eminent debate program at Emory, the Barkley Forum. These are two of the forty-nine awards from 1962 through 2013, while eleven others went to medical faculty members and thirty to arts and sciences faculty members (both of these faculties number many hundreds). Law had two, public health three, and business none.

Similarly, the Scholar/Teacher Award is given at commencement each year, courtesy of The United Methodist Church Board of Higher Education and Ministry. It recognizes a faculty member who excels in teaching, demonstrates strong mentoring of students, and contributes significantly to the scholarly life of the university. From 1981 through 2013, three Candler faculty members received the award: Don E. Saliers (1999), James W. Fowler (2005), and E. Brooks Holifield (2010). (One other recipient, William Beardslee, the first recipient, had tenure in the Emory College Department of Religion but played a prominent role in teaching New Testament studies in the Graduate Division of Religion.) All of this is so, even as the theology school faculty in proportion to the total university faculty has declined over the years, from 5 percent in 1920 (8 of 159 faculty members) to 2.45 percent in 1950 to less than 1 percent in 1980.

Despite the diminishing numerical proportion of the theology faculty in the university, the sway of the theology faculty in the governance of the university has been significant. In the seventeen years from 1987 to 2004, four Candler faculty members served as president of the University Senate and one served as secretary. And during part of this time, one—James Laney—served as university president.

Of 194 Emory Medal recipients since the inception of the honor in 1946, 9 represented Candler. Of the 175 "Makers of History" recognized by Emory at its 175th anniversary convocation in December 2011, 22 had been associated in some way with Candler—either as alumni or as leaders of the school or as transformative philanthropists.

During the 2005–12 Emory Campaign to raise $1.6 billion for the university, Candler had a goal of $60 million—which it reached a year ahead of schedule; in the end, Candler raised $65.4 million. As of the end of fiscal year 2012, the part of the Emory endowment dedicated to Candler (that is, designated by donors for use by Candler) ranked third among those for all schools at Emory (behind the medical school and Emory College), although it is younger than three of the schools and has a smaller alumni base than most. Moreover, its alumni enter traditionally less lucrative fields than alumni of, say, the schools of medicine, law, and business.

Academically, Candler has a reputation that places it among the top schools of theology in the country. Even as long ago as 1965, the Association of Theological Schools ranked it fifth among university-related seminaries. In 1996 the National Research Council released its occasional report on graduate education in the United States; the Emory University Graduate Division of Religion, which awards the PhD degree in the James T. Laney School of Graduate Studies (named, of course, for the former theology dean and university president), and the majority of whose faculty have their tenure home in Candler, was ranked among the top five programs in religion nationwide.

Emory history helps to make sense of a lot of these measures of the excellence and impact of Candler. Founded in 1836 by a church body, Emory College flourished for eighty-three years in a community whose ethos would have fit a camp meeting as much as a town. The college was devoted to theological and biblical instruction as well as to the classic liberal arts, and its tone of preparing young men for service to

Before contributions by the theology faculty, the Emory University Museum was known for stuffed birds, arrowheads, shells, a cabinet full of gems and other rock samples, and the oldest Maytag washer in Georgia.

the common good easily carried over to the new university when it was chartered in 1915. The university itself grew out of a church controversy, and as a consequence the church paid close attention to its relationship to Emory, especially by attending to the theology school.

Well into the middle of the twentieth century, Emory presidents were all devoted Methodists, and the first four leaders of the new university in Atlanta—Bishop Candler and presidents Harvey Cox, Goodrich White, and S. Walter Martin—all were elected to jurisdictional or general conferences of their denomination. The first board chair of the newly chartered university, in 1915, Asa Candler, was almost as devout a Methodist as his brother Warren and helped to found Wesley Memorial Hospital in downtown Atlanta—later Emory University Hospital. Asa's successor in chairing the board was his oldest son, Charles Howard Candler Sr., who, with his wife, Flora Glenn Candler, gave most of the funds to build Glenn Memorial Methodist Church on the Emory campus in memory of her father, Wilbur Fisk Glenn, a Methodist minister and Emory alumnus (class of 1861).

Charles Candler's successor as board chair was Henry Bowden Sr., a founding member of the Committee of One Hundred. As board chair, Bowden made up one-third of the troika that ran the university for the year between the presidencies of Walter Martin and Sanford Atwood; the second member of the team was retired president and chancellor (and Methodist) Goodrich White, and the third was Judson C. "Jake" Ward 33C 36G. Ward served in various positions of authority at Emory for decades and taught a Sunday school class at Glenn Memorial for fifty years. Clearly the university reflected in countless ways the religious and social outlook of its church-bred founders. Naturally the school of theology both contributed to and benefitted from this emphasis.

# Candler and Emory, Take Two

Beyond helping to shape the ethos of the university, the theology school has contributed immeasurably to the intellectual and cultural resources of Emory in two quite concrete ways: through the nurturing of a first-rate museum and through the building of the first real research library at Emory. (For a thorough history of the Pitts Theology Library, see chapter 7.)

## Bird Carcasses, Mummies, and Art

The front page of the *Atlanta Journal* for February 11, 1923, carried an article written by the future author of *Gone with the Wind*, whose byline on that Sunday was "Peggy Mitchell." The article recounted the adventures of a Candler School of Theology professor, a kind of Indiana Jones in the valley of the tombs. "Theology Professor Just Missed Tutankhamen," the headline proclaimed. Indeed, William A. Shelton, one of the first faculty members at Candler, had gone to Egypt and Palestine in 1920 at the invitation of the eminent biblical archaeologist J. H. Breasted. The founding director of the Oriental Institute at the University of Chicago, Breasted was perhaps the preeminent archaeologist of his day. Shelton, one of Breasted's former students, was the only scholar not from the University of Chicago invited on the trip.

Shelton himself recounts his fascinating journey through present-day Iraq, Syria, Israel, and Egypt in his 1922 book, *Dust and Ashes of Empires*, and Andrew W. M. Beierle tells the broader story of Shelton's life in "One Brick from Babylon," in *Emory Magazine* (October 1988: 8–18). Newly liberated from the Ottoman Empire after World War I, the region was open to Western scholarly exploration for the first time in centuries, and the lack of restrictions on recovering and exporting antiquities at the time meant that Breasted's "American Scientific Mission," as it was called, could send home crates of materials. And they did.

The treasures that Shelton discovered included a lipstick holder that had belonged to the grandmother of King Tut's wife. But while Shelton stood in the tomb of Ramesses III, directly over Tut's as-yet-undiscovered tomb in 1920, he never dreamed of what lay beneath his feet. He later remarked that he was more disappointed in not happening on Tut's (almost) final resting place than in anything else in his life. Still, if it was unfortunate that Howard Carter, not Shelton, found the tomb of the Boy Pharaoh (what would that collection have done to the university's endowment?), in some respects Shelton found something almost as valuable—a seed. It was a seed comprising the materials he shipped back to Atlanta, which would serve as the beginning of what is now the Michael C. Carlos Museum, one of the premier university museums in the South.

Shelton did not actually beget the museum, which predated his contributions to it. Emory College had collected an assortment of odds and ends through the latter half of the nineteenth century and used the word "museum" as much out of aspiration as for description. There were stuffed birds, arrowheads, shells, a cabinet full of gems and other rock samples, and, according to one commentator, "Georgia's oldest Maytag washing machine." One can see the remnants of this collection in the John Huston film *Wise Blood*, when two characters wander into what was then called the Sociology Building (now Carlos Hall) to view the shrunken remnants of a boneless and mummified man (a figment of Flannery O'Connor's imagination, not an actual part of the museum's collection).

But Shelton set the course for what would take shape over the next decades. Collecting at a time when Egyptian and international law was far more lax about the dispatriation of antiquities than it is today, Shelton garnered much. The bill of lading for his shipment of Middle Eastern archaeological materials includes some 250 artifacts, from Egyptian mummies and coffins to Babylonian stamps and Palestinian potsherds. With these treasures on display, the Emory University Museum soon became, in the nomenclature of visiting schoolchildren, "The Mummy Museum."

The reputation of Emory for housing mummies gained renewed energy in 1999, when the museum director, Anthony Hirschel, seized an opportunity presented by the closing of the Niagara Falls Museum and Daredevil Hall of Fame, in Niagara Falls, Canada. By then the Emory museum had gained the patronage (and the name) of Michael C. Carlos and his wife, Thalia Carlos, and the Emory collections had diversified significantly to include Greek and Roman antiquities, pre-Columbian art of the Americas, photographs, and other works on paper.

When the Niagara Falls Museum put up its going-out-of-business sign, the curator of Egyptian antiquities at Emory, Peter Lacovara, called the sale to Hirschel's attention. With seven days to raise the $2 million asking price, Hirschel turned to the Atlanta community for help. Carlos advisory board chairman James Miller and his wife, Karina Lichirie Miller 61C, put up half the funds, and another $750,000 was contributed by donors ranging from schoolchildren to Emory staff members—enough to secure a commitment from the museum to sell the 145 artifacts to Emory.

Among the ten mummies that arrived on campus later that year was one that had lain in Niagara Falls since 1860. The mummy's profile resembled those of two mummies resting in a museum in Cairo, Egypt—Seti I and Ramesses II (Ramesses the Great, the pharaoh of the book of Exodus). These were the son and grandson of Ramesses I. With technology ranging from CT scans and X-rays to radiocarbon dating, the mummy was determined with almost certainty to be that of Ramesses I. In 2003 Emory returned Ramesses I to Egypt, where he now lies in state in the Egyptian Museum in Cairo's Tahrir Square.

## CANDLER AND EMORY, TAKE THREE

By a strange coincidence, ninety-seven years to the day after the Tennessee Supreme Court provided the impetus for the Methodist Episcopal Church, South, to cut its ties to Vanderbilt University, a student at Emory University published a newspaper editorial suggesting that it was time for Emory to cut its ties with its own theology school.

The student first suggested that any subject left over from the Middle Ages should be jettisoned, on the analogy that modern science has left behind alchemy and astrology. Thus, theology should be tossed out the door. What the student overlooked was that alchemy and astrology were never central to the medieval university, while theology—along with law and medicine—lay at the heart of education in Bologna and Paris and Oxford. No one would suggest that Emory should cease teaching law and medicine, let alone the ancient liberal arts, just because they were taught five hundred years ago.

But something else was gnawing at the student, and it is possible that he was merely voicing what often is thought but left unsaid—a belief that any theology school is likely to be out of step with the intellectual rigor of the rest of a modern university. Somehow, perhaps (this feeling suggests), the theology curriculum is more dogmatic and dependent on "revealed truth," while other schools and disciplines can be subjected to critical questioning. Theology schools, in this view, have not shed either their obedience to authority or the fuzziness of their feel-good mission to make the world a happier place.

Only someone who has never sat in a Candler course or had a thoroughgoing conversation with a faculty member there would make this assumption. From its beginning, the Candler School of Theology has never scheduled indoctrination sessions on the academic calendar (what happens in regular chapel services may be different). In reality, as any alumnus of Candler might confess, theology schools harbor as much doubt and skepticism as any department in a liberal arts college or in other professional schools. And even those other schools and departments are not immune to their own forms of faith or dogmatism. In truth, most theology students show no more reverence for the authority of their churches than do, say, medical students for the practices of the residency system or law students for the monopoly of the American Bar Association.

Indeed, schools of theology often are places where men and women exhibit great intellectual courage, from Martin Luther to Martin Luther King Jr. The dogmatisms of secular principalities and powers need not be spared critique from outside secularism's own system of belief.

Some might argue that a theology school should be abolished because its function could be filled by any number of departments elsewhere in the university. If that were true, one might just as well close schools of public health, nursing, or law in favor of melding their curricula with those of colleges. But professional schools, like those for theology, are not about intellect only. They are about the shaping of professional practices, professional habits, and ways of viewing the world through the particular lenses necessary for a profession.

What, then, are the rigors of professional training in theology—comparable to training in medicine or law—that justify its perpetuation at a university like Emory? And what makes it desirable for any research university to harbor a place for theological education?

The short answer to the second question is that religion is not going to disappear as a human phenomenon. So it behooves the university to help men and women understand more clearly religion's place in modern life. But the university also does the converse; it shines a light on the way modern life affects religious practice. That is, Candler applies all the tools of modern scholarship—from postmodern thought to statistical modeling, from archival research to institutional review boards—in preparing men and women to help address the endemic ills of the spirit suffered by modern men and women.

These ills are no less real—whatever their source—than the ills addressed by those studying in schools of public health or nursing or medicine. Nor is the theology graduate's mode of addressing them necessarily less effective than the modes of graduates from other professional schools. Some research, in fact, suggests that in meeting the public health needs of the world, graduates of theology schools can

serve as important allies to graduates of public health schools. How are public health students to learn these things without theological allies in their university?

The distinctive feature of a theology school that makes it worthy of its place in the university is its capacity to train people in a particular way of knowing—the feature of each professional school. In the case of theology, it is a way of knowing that no religion department is prepared to undertake and no arts and sciences college could perform. It is the blend of the practitioner's craft with the scholar's knowledge. An analogy might reside in the kind of learning that takes place in a school of music, in an MFA program in poetry, or in science labs where textbook knowledge and some degree of artistic competence come together. To suggest that the rest of the university has nothing to learn from any of these ways of knowing is a form of intellectual smugness that has no place in a university.

As the Candler School of Theology begins its second century, may it be guided by intellectual humility, even as it continues its mission: "grounded in the Christian faith and shaped by the Wesleyan tradition of evangelical piety, ecumenical openness, and social concern . . . to educate—through scholarship, teaching, and service—faithful and creative leaders for the church's ministries in the world."

# CANDLER MAKERS OF HISTORY

In 2011 Emory University celebrated the 175th anniversary of the founding of Emory College on December 10, 1836. Among the commemorative activities of the "quartoseptcentennial" year, the Emory Alumni Association charged a committee of alumni and institutional historians to identify 175 Emory men and women who had made history, either while at Emory or after graduating from it. Twenty of the "makers of history" had an association with the Candler School of Theology (they actually include 23 individuals, but married couples and the Indigo Girls were counted only as 1 each of the 175).

Below, in alphabetical order, are the Candler people who helped make Emory history.

**Jack Boozer 40C 42T—Professor of Religion**

As the Charles Howard Candler Professor of Religion in Emory College for more than thirty-five years, Boozer was an Emory legend, beloved by generations of students. Following his graduation from Emory College and the Candler School of Theology, he served as an ordained Methodist minister in the U.S. Army chaplaincy, and the work of the military chaplain became a focus of much of his publishing activity. An award-winning teacher of Christian theology, Boozer joined colleagues in the theology school and elsewhere at Emory in calling for racial integration of Emory in the 1950s. As an aggressive advocate for the emerging profile of Emory as an institution aspiring to educate ethical leadership, he engaged in many of the issues of social justice in Atlanta. In fostering interfaith dialogue, he was instrumental in establishing the Jay and Leslie Cohen Chair of Judaic Studies and helped to develop University Worship and the ethics program in the School of Medicine. He received from Emory its highest faculty honor, the Thomas Jefferson Award, as well as the Emory Williams Award for teaching.

**Henry Morton Bullock 24C 25T—Historian of Emory**

Born in 1902 in Chicago, Bullock made Emory history by writing it. After graduating from Emory College and the theology school, he went on to earn a PhD from Yale University, writing the first full-length account of the development of his alma mater for his doctoral dissertation. He revised the work in order to publish it as *A History of Emory University* in time for the Emory centennial in 1936. A Methodist clergyman and educator, Bullock taught English at Blackburn College, in Illinois, and later served as professor and chair of the Department of Religion at Millsaps College, in Mississippi. He wrote many books and essays and served the last decade and a half of his career as an editor of Methodist publications in Nashville. A typescript of his Emory history and accompanying correspondence are part of the Manuscript, Archives, and Rare Book Library (MARBL) at Emory.

## Asa Griggs Candler—Coca-Cola Founder; Philanthropist; Emory Board Chair

Although he never earned an Emory degree, Asa Candler can legitimately stake a claim as one of the half-dozen most important contributors to Emory history. In 1888 he bought the formula (and the rights) for Coca-Cola from its inventor, John Pemberton, and took the first step in changing the history of Atlanta and the South. Under his guidance, The Coca-Cola Company grew into one of the most prosperous enterprises in the region. Devout in his Methodism, and taking to heart Wesley's admonition to "give all that you can," Candler shared his wealth with Atlanta and wielded positive influence as businessman, mayor, philanthropist, and church leader. He bought land to help head off a real estate slump; he lent money to desperate cotton growers until prices rose; he averted a crisis in city government by agreeing to serve as mayor in 1917; he provided the lion's share

of funding when the North Georgia Conference of the Methodist Episcopal Church, South (MECS), founded Wesley Memorial Hospital (later Emory University Hospital) in Atlanta. Candler took a special interest in the small denominational college called Emory, in Oxford, Georgia, and in 1914 he donated $1 million and seventy-five acres to help it become part of the new university in Atlanta. He served as chair of the Emory board of trustees for more than a quarter of a century. By the time of his death in 1929 he had given some $8 million to Emory, a staggering sum for the time.

## Warren Akin Candler 1875C 35H—President and Chancellor of Emory; Methodist Bishop

Even if he had never invited his brother, Asa, to become engaged in Emory College, Warren Candler would have had a major impact on Emory. As Emory College president from 1888 to 1898, Candler worked diligently to make the college debt-free, raising money for new buildings and contributing his own modest resources toward a student loan fund and the endowment. One of his most enduring legacies at his alma mater, however, grew out of his attitude toward athletics. Persuaded that intercollegiate sports distracted students from their first responsibility

and fostered gambling, Candler persuaded the trustees to ban intercollegiate sports and instead promoted "athletics for all" through one of the nation's first successful organized intramural sports programs. In 1898

Candler was elected a bishop in the Methodist Episcopal Church, South (MECS), becoming in time the leading conservative voice in Southern Methodism. After the MECS severed ties with Vanderbilt University, Bishop Candler chaired the committee that oversaw the creation of a new university in the Southeast and the incorporation of Emory College into it. He served as chancellor of Emory University from 1914 to 1920.

## Ernest Cadman Colwell 23C 27T 44H—President, University of Chicago; Founding Director, Emory's Institute of Liberal Arts

A native Georgian, Colwell went on from Emory College and the Candler School of Theology to earn a PhD from the University of Chicago in 1930, when he was invited to join the faculty there. For more than two decades he served the University of Chicago in many roles, including as president. In 1951 President Goodrich White recruited Colwell to Emory as vice president and dean of faculties—many thought as a way of grooming him to succeed White, who would retire in 1957. At Emory Colwell founded the Graduate Institute of the Liberal Arts, developed somewhat on the model of the Committee on Social Thought at Chicago. He chaired the executive committee of the International Greek New Testament Project at Emory and chaired the board of trustees of the Interdenominational Theological Center in Atlanta. When the Emory trustees turned elsewhere to find White's successor as president, Colwell left Emory in 1957 to become president of the Claremont School of Theology in California, establishing the school on a new campus after it had separated from the University of Southern California the previous year.

## John Lloyd Cromartie 64C 88T—Attorney; Minister

Following his education at Emory College, Cromartie enrolled at the University of Georgia School of Law, where he served as a law review editor and garnered many prizes. Before launching his career in law, he clerked for U.S. District Court judge Sidney O. Smith Jr., and he went on to  argue cases at the highest levels, including the U.S. Supreme Court. For a time he was executive director of the statewide Georgia Legal Services Program, which provides free legal clinics to low-income clients. Responding to a call to the ministry, Cromartie earned his MDiv at Candler while winning numerous student awards. He went on to serve for many years as senior pastor of First United Methodist Church in Cumming, Georgia, frequently writing for and teaching many audiences on the topic of faith and the law.

## Neal Bond Fleming 33C 36T—Dean, Oxford College

Fleming served as dean of Oxford College of Emory University from 1966 until his retirement in 1978. He led a decade of growth on the campus, which saw the addition of a library and athletic facilities as well as renovation of Candler Hall into a student center. Working to es-  tablish a solid financial foundation for Oxford, Fleming strengthened the ties of the two-year school to the rest of Emory and coined the term "continuees" for those Oxford graduates who go on to Emory College to complete their bachelor's degrees. He established the Oxford Board of Counselors, which continues to serve as vital contributors to the college in both advisory and philanthropic ways. In retirement, Fleming and his wife, Mary Louise, continued to be active in the life of the college and community, and in 1987 Fleming came out of retirement to serve as interim dean for a year. An ordained Methodist minister he helped to found the Oxford Historical Shrine Society and worked to raise funds to restore Old Church. He died in June 2009 at age ninety-nine.

## Susan T. Henry-Crowe 76T—First Female President of The United Methodist Church Judicial Council

A member of the South Carolina Conference of  The United Methodist Church, Henry-Crowe was appointed chaplain of Emory University in 1991 and was later named dean of the chapel and religious life. For more than two decades her focus on fostering interreligious dialogue at Emory—coordinating the work of more than two dozen student religious groups of all the world's major faiths—served as a model for other institutions of higher education and helped establish a distinctive tone and ethos for religious discourse on campus. Elected in 1992 to her first eight-year term on the Judicial Council, the denomination's "supreme court," she stepped off for four years before being elected to a second term in 2004 and became the president of the council in 2008. In 2000 The United Methodist Foundation for Christian Higher Education named her Chaplain of the Year. She used the five-thousand-dollar award to help fund the Emory Journeys Program, which takes Emory students and faculty to regions of the world that have experienced trouble and strife in order to learn more about the roots of conflict and the possibilities of peace. In 2014 she began service as executive director of the United Methodist General Board of Church and Society in Washington, DC.

## Indigo Girls, Amy Ray 86C and Emily Saliers 85C—Grammy-Winning Musicians

Although not officially schooled by the Candler School of Theology, Emily Saliers breathed its atmosphere as the daughter of Professor Don Saliers and passed along some of that influence to her fellow Emory collegian,

Amy Ray. The two met in high school and began performing together as the Indigo Girls before graduating from Emory. Always keeping their alma mater close to their hearts, Ray and Saliers frequently return to campus to speak and perform; in September 2010 the Indigo Girls headlined the Emory Homecoming concert and played to a crowd of thousands on McDonough Field. With her father, Emily published the book *A Song to Sing, a Life to Live: Reflections on Music as Spiritual Practice* (1986).

## L. Bevel Jones III 46C 49T 97H—Methodist Bishop

When he enrolled at Emory College, Jones began a six-decades-plus relationship with his university. After earning his undergraduate degree from the college and his MDiv from Candler, he served six pastorates in North Georgia, the same conference that his father had served for half a century and that his son David 76T would later serve. Along the way Bevel Jones remained active as a Candler alumnus and would be elected to the Emory board of trustees, which he would serve for a decade as vice chair. He was one of eighty-eight religious leaders in Atlanta who signed the famous "Ministers' Manifesto" of 1957, urging that Georgia schools remain open during desegregation. Elected to the episcopacy in 1984 he served the Charlotte area until his retirement in 1996.

## Arthur B. Keys 92T—Founder and CEO of International Relief and Development

A graduate of Bethany College and Yale Divinity School, Keys had established a successful career in relief work before earning his DMin from Candler. His work had taken him from the executive directorship of Interfaith Impact for Justice and Peace to service as secretary of public ministries for the United Church Board for Homeland Ministries and to work through his own consulting firm, International Relief and Development (IRD), which he founded in 1998. IRD distributed more than $1.75 billion in humanitarian assistance over the next decade to Asia, Africa, Latin America, Eastern Europe, the Middle East, and the U.S. Gulf Coast. In addition to domestic and international humanitarian assistance, IRD provides economic development and programs in food and agriculture self-sufficiency.

## Nelia J. 74T and R. Calvin Kimbrough 75T—Humanitarians

The Kimbroughs enrolled in Candler School of Theology in 1971 and liked the place so much they decided to stay on after completing their MDivs—Nelia as assistant dean for Student Academic Services and Calvin as founding director of the media center. In 1977, along with two other couples, they founded Patchwork Central, an inner-city program in Evansville, Indiana, that has touched the lives of thousands. The Kimbroughs remained at Patchwork Central for twenty-seven years, directing its commu-

nity outreach programs and living, working, and worshipping in the neighborhood. In 2004 they left Patchwork Central to work at Atlanta's Open Door Community and continue much the same ministry among the people of Atlanta. This residential community serves meals, staffs a free medical clinic, conducts worship services and meetings, and provides a prison ministry.

## James T. Laney 94H—Dean of Candler; President of Emory; U.S. Ambassador to Korea

An ordained Methodist minister, Laney taught at Yonsei University in Korea and Vanderbilt University before becoming dean of Candler School of Theology, where he served from 1969 to 1977. Appointed to the Emory presidency in 1977, in his first

annual report to the board he outlined steps he wanted to take to improve undergraduate life at Emory: increasing scholarship funds to attract the best students, enhancing residence and dining facilities, providing adequate recreation facilities, and emphasizing collaboration among the disciplines. Laney served as U.S. ambassador to South Korea from 1993 to 1997 and helped defuse the nuclear crisis with North Ko-

rea in 1994. In 2009 the graduate school at Emory was named the James T. Laney School for Graduate Studies.

## J. Marvin Rast 18C 29T—Author of Alma Mater Lyrics

Rast was among the last of the Emory College students to graduate from the school while it was still in Oxford, Georgia. Going on to a career as a Methodist minister and educator (he was president of Lander College in South Carolina from 1941 to 1948), he wrote a religiously themed, syndicated column, "Altar Stairs," for thirty years. But as far as Emory is concerned his  work never could surpass the fame he achieved with his pen during his senior year in college. Following a Men's Glee Club practice in the spring of 1918, the director, Christian Hamff, lamented the absence of a distinctively Emory song. Hearing this, Rast took inspiration, retreated to his dorm, and wrote the lyrics that became the Emory alma mater. While the tune is all-too-familiar and hardly distinctive to Emory ("Far above Cayuga's Waters," sung at Cornell and countless other schools and colleges), the hymn made its debut at Rast's own graduation in 1918 and has undergone slight modifications since, to take account of admission of women and changing mores in Dixie.

## O. Wayne 86H and Grace Crum Rollins 95H— Business Leaders; Philanthropists

Signaling the importance of the Rollins family to Emory is nearly impossible. Growing up in Northwest Georgia and working long hours in a cotton field during the Great Depression, Wayne Rollins never went to college. Yet through drive, acumen, and good business sense, he built one of the world's largest service companies and became one of the richest men in America, according to *Forbes* magazine. As a Methodist interested in strengthening the gifts and graces of clergy in small towns and rural areas of his state, he directed his first gifts to Emory University to the Candler School of Theology, which established the Rollins Center for Church Ministries. In 1990 he saw the newly formed School of Public Health at Emory as a vehicle for reaching out to underserved communities, and his support helped build what is now the Rollins School of Public Health. Wayne's wife, Grace, continued his good works following his death in 1991. In all, five generations of Rollinses have relationships with Emory. The Rita Anne Rollins Building—named in memory of Wayne and Grace's first grandchild, who died tragically young—became the home to the Candler School of Theology in 2008.

## Kiyoshi Tanimoto 40T 86H—Theologian; Founder, Hiroshima Peace Center Foundation

On August 6, 1945, the minister of the Nagarehawa United Church of Christ in Hiroshima, Japan, was going about his ministerial rounds when the first use of an atomic bomb in wartime was unleashed. That bomb destroyed his church and killed scores of his parishioners. The minister, Kiyoshi Tanimoto, was a graduate of the Candler School of Theology. He survived the bombing and spent weeks helping his parish and his city to recover and rebuild. Indeed, he devoted the rest of his life to helping other survivors. Most prominent among those survivors were the "Hiroshima Maidens," twenty-five young women who had been terribly disfigured by the blast. After the war, Tanimoto toured the United States to raise money for their care as well as other peace projects. Offered an honorary degree as part of the Emory sesquicentennial observance in 1986, Tanimoto was preparing to return to the Emory campus when he was taken unexpectedly by death. His wife received the degree on his behalf.

## Barbara Brown Taylor 73C—Priest; Preacher; Author

Following graduation from Emory, Taylor went off to Yale Divinity School and then returned to hometown Atlanta to prepare for ordination in the Episcopal Church. In the meantime she needed a job—and Candler needed her, as assistant to the dean. Soon enough she went off to a little church in the mountains and began to gain renown. In 1996 Baylor University named her one of the twelve most effective preachers in the English-speaking world. (Billy Graham was another, but so were three others who had Candler connections—Fred Craddock and Tom Long, who both taught preaching at Candler, and William Willimon, who earned his doctoral degree from Candler in 1973 and later served Emory as a trustee.) Accepting an invitation to teach religion at Piedmont College, in Northeast Georgia, she also served as an adjunct professor at Columbia Theological Seminary in Decatur. She was named Georgia Author of the Year in 2006, and her twelfth book, *An Altar in the World*, made *The New York Times* best seller list.

## James Turpin 49C 51T 55M—Founder, Project Concern International

It is a curious thing how many graduates of theology school feel called to care for bodies as well as souls. So it was with James Turpin, who followed his theology degree by entering the Emory University School of Medicine. Six years after earning his MD, while serving as a young doctor in San Diego, Turpin volunteered some time at a Tijuana clinic, where he saved the lives of two small children who were dying of pneumonia. That experience led him to create Project Concern International (PCI), which has forever changed the lives of millions of children and families around the world. From setting up volunteer-run health clinics in the developing world to establishing PCI's "Walks for Mankind" across North America, Turpin and his organization have helped millions of people live healthier, more sustainable, and more hopeful lives.

## Melissa Maxcy Wade 72C 76G 96T 00T—Barkley Forum Leader

Debate has been a tradition and strength at Emory since the earliest days of the college, when students created the Phi Gamma and Few "literary societies" as

a focus of campus life— organizations that combined the benefits and some of the liabilities of fraternities, debate teams, eating clubs, and libraries. By 1950 the societies had been disbanded and morphed into the Emory Debate Club, which in that year was named the Barkley Forum in honor of U.S. vice president Alben W. Barkley, 1900C. In 1959 Glenn Pelham took over the leadership of the Barkley Forum, and within eight years the program had won its first national championship. When Pelham retired in 1972, Wade, one of his top debaters, took over. Since then, Emory debaters have won more than twenty national team championships and individual champion speaker awards, including the National Debate Tournament in 2010 and 2011. Wade also led in establishing the nationally renowned Urban Debate Leagues (UDLs), which offer debate opportunities to inner-city youth. Today, thirty-five thousand students and teachers take part in twenty-three UDLs nationwide.

## James M. Wall 49C 55T 85H—Editor, *The Christian Century*

As an Emory undergraduate, Wall was the associate editor of the *Emory Wheel* and worked full time as a sportswriter for the *Atlanta Journal*, so his later career in church-related journalism started in Druid Hills. Indeed, he was well on his way to a writing career when, in

1952, following service in the military, he returned to Emory as a Candler student. After serving pastorates in small Georgia towns for a number of years, he was able in time to merge his two vocations of journalism and ministry by editing Methodist publications. In 1972 he became editor of the *Christian Century*, the publication viewed by many as the flagship of mainline Protestantism, where for twenty-seven years he played a major role in the dialogue on ethical and religious concern within Protestant denominations. After stepping down as editor, Wall continued as a contributing editor for the publication.

## CHAPTER ONE

**P. 2 $25,000 . . . about what it paid in legal costs for its lawsuit**
Paul K. Conklin, *Gone with the Ivy: A Biography of Vanderbilt University* (Knoxville: University of Tennessee Press, 1985), 181

**P. 6 American university . . . suited the aims of a denomination like Methodism**
Glenn T. Miller, *Piety and Profession: American Protestant Theological Education, 1870–1970* (Grand Rapids: Wm. B. Eerdmans, 2007), 225

**P. 7 Giant Against the Sky**
Alfred M. Pierce, *Giant Against the Sky: The Life of Bishop Warren Akin Candler* (New York: Abingdon-Cokesbury Press, 1948)

**P. 7 he opposed what he called "soap and soup religion"**
Pierce, 244–45

**P. 7 a "return to Wesley's God"**
Pierce, 247

**P. 8 the cosmic soul, the cosmic God, the cosmic Christ,**
Boone M. Bowen, *The Candler School of Theology: Sixty Years of Service* (Atlanta: Emory University, 1974), 168

**P. 8 Durham . . . cofounder of the Commission on Interracial Cooperation**
Bowen, 169; see also David Fort Godshalk, *Veiled Visions: The 1906 Atlanta Race Riot and the Reshaping of American Race Relations* (Chapel Hill: University of North Carolina Press, 2005), 264

**P. 10 they were successful preachers**
Wyatt Aiken Smart, "They Accused the Bishop of Heresy," *The Emory Alumnus* (October 1957): 17

**P. 10 "almost to a man students of Andrew Sledd"**
Gary S. Hauk and Sally Wolff King, eds., *Where Courageous Inquiry Leads: The Emerging Life of Emory University* (Atlanta: Emory University and Bookhouse Group, 2010), 38

**P. 13 of whom 59 had graduated**
Emory University Board of Trustees, Minutes, June 9, 1917

**P. 13 in the fall of 1918, the enrollment fell to 77**
Emory University Board of Trustees, Minutes, June 7, 1919

**P. 13 fall of 1918 also brought the resignation of Dean Durham**
Bowen, 31–32

## CHAPTER TWO

**P. 15 As the churches in America made the transition from the Progressive Era**
Miller, 381

**P. 17 The Fundamentals, a twelve-volume series of essays**
Ernest Robert Sandeen, *The Roots of Fundamentalism: British and American Millenarianism, 1800–1930* (Chicago: University of Chicago Press, 2008), 197

**P. 17 The term "fundamentalist" itself was coined as the new decade began.**
George M. Marsden, *Fundamentalism and American Culture* (New York: Oxford University Press, 2006), 119

**P. 18 "making harmony between mind and heart."**
Franklin N. Parker, *What We Believe: Studies in Christian Doctrine* (Nashville: Publishing House Methodist Episcopal Church, South, 1924), 5–6

**P. 19 the doctrine [of the atonement] under the conditions of its own time**
Parker, 31

**P. 21 widespread indifference, if not opposition, to specific theological education**
Franklin N. Parker, quoted in Emory University President's Report to the Board of Trustees, 1929

**P. 21 difficulty growing out of the alleged liberalism of the views and teachings of certain professors**
Parker, quoted in Emory University President's Report to the Board of Trustees, 1929

**P. 21 literary criticism, historical criticism, and form criticism**
Wyatt Aiken Smart, *The Contemporary Christ: The Fondren Lectures for 1942* (New York, Nashville: Abingdon-Cokesbury Press, 1942)

**P. 22 "to let the past speak to the present without enslaving it."**
Wyatt Aiken Smart, *Still the Bible Speaks* (New York: Abingdon-Cokesbury Press, 1948)

**P. 23 Southern Methodism experienced less fundamentalist enthusiasm**
Miller, 437-40

**P. 23 In 1844 the president of Emory College's board of trustees**
For the fullest account of slave-holding by early Emory trustees and faculty members, see Mark Auslander, *The Accidental Slaveowner: Revisiting a Myth of Race and Finding an American Family* (Athens: University of Georgia Press, 2011)

**P. 26 Non-Methodist students were not even admitted until 1935**
Bowen, 66

**P. 27 enrollment grew to 142 in the fall of 1941**
Emory University President's Report to the Board of Trustees, 1941

## CHAPTER THREE

**P. 31 "the correct use of the English language."**
Bulletins of the Candler School of Theology, 1915–30, Manuscript, Archives, and Rare Book Library, Emory University

**P. 33 Candler School of Theology must develop in stride with the University**
Henry Burton Trimble, quoted in Emory University President's Report to the Board of Trustees, 1938–39

**P. 34 the arrest of a Candler student— Tatsumasa Shirakawa, a native of Japan**
Bowen, 192

**P. 34 memorandum from the Justice Department to J. Edgar Hoover**
See http://www.foitimes.com/internment/Arrest01.pdf

**P. 35 Hoke S. Bell**
Letter quoted in Bowen, 62

**P. 37 the theology school would have a hard time keeping pace**
Miller, 665

**P. 38 resembled a plan instituted shortly after the war at Perkins**
Miller, 696

**P. 38 a study of some eminently successful pastors**
Bulletins of the Candler School of Theology, 1930–44, Manuscript, Archives, and Rare Book Library, Emory University

**P. 41 Protestant Radio and Television Center**
See Bowen, 88–90, and http://day1
.org/2243-historic_protestant_hour_
archives_to_be_restored

**P. 42 vocational aptitude, . . . psychological state and . . . level of cultural attainment**
Bowen, 80

**P. 42 Growing by 1950 to become the third-largest Methodist seminary**
Emory University President's Report to the Board of Trustees, 1950.

CHAPTER FOUR

**P. 46 preferred the fiction of Walter Scott over that of Mark Twain**
Williams Ragsdale Cannon, *A Magnificent Obsession: The Autobiography of William Ragsdale Cannon* (Nashville: Abingdon Press, 1999), 36

**P. 55 in Weber's recollection, "stone-walled us the whole time"**
"The School of Theology as Prelude: Candler Conversations—Manfred Hoffmann, William Mallard, Theodore Runyon, and Theodore Weber," in Hauk and King, 164

**P. 56 The resolution hit a brick wall in the board of trustees.**
For a full account of the integration movement at Emory in the 1950s and 1960s, see Melissa F. Kean, "National Ambition, Regional Turmoil: The Desegregation of Emory," in Hauk and King, 39–55; and Kean, "'At a Most Uncomfortable Speed': The Desegregation of the South's Private Universities, 1945–1964" (PhD dissertation, Rice University, 2000), 276–77

**P. 57 Cannon . . . witnessed the elimination of racial discrimination.**
Bowen, 116

**P. 58 underestimate income and overestimate expenses**
Cannon, 168

**P. 58 he was not a seminal . . . scholar in the view of some of his faculty**
See Hauk and King, 164. Professor Emeritus William Mallard notes that Cannon's *History of Christianity in the Middle Ages* is "a summary of known materials" and not "a new reading of primary sources." Cannon "did not consistently show a scholarly mind." Mallard also credits Cannon's "strong logical mind"

**P. 62 God is not dead at Emory. He is very much alive**
Cannon, 177–78

**P. 63 a chance to do for our century something of what Thomas did for his**
William Mallard, letter to Ralph McGill, publisher of the *Atlanta Constitution*, July 3, 1966, in William Mallard Papers (MSS 336), Pitts Theology Library archives

**P. 63 genuinely open to a variety of approaches, interests, and concerns**
Hauk and King, 167

**P. 64 Emory was a truly radical center, or surely it was so theologically**
Thomas J. J. Altizer, *Living the Death of God: A Theological Memoir* (New York: State University of New York Press, 2006), 9

CHAPTER FIVE

**P. 69 Bishop Candler's animus against feminism**
Emory University Board of Trustees minutes, June 7, 1919

**P. 69 Job Analysis of a Mother of Preschool Children**
Mary Vaughn Johnson (Mrs. Emmett), "Job Analysis of a Mother of Preschool Children, as Indicated by Eight Mothers Whose Husbands Were Students in the Candler School of Theology Summer 1936" (BD dissertation, Candler School of Theology, Emory University, 1938), Pitts Theology Library Special Collections

**P. 69 mid-1940s, women began enrolling in greater numbers**
Bowen, 209–46

**P. 71 Dean Laney reported that enrollment for the fall of 1970**
Annual Report of the Candler School of Theology, 1970, 1971, 1978

**P. 71 noncredit program "designed to help women adjust" to the role of "minister's wife."**
"Theology School to Train Ministers' Wives," *The Emory Alumnus* (February 1973): 9

**P. 73 first women . . . in faculty or faculty-like positions began appearing in Dean Laney's administration.**
Bulletins of the Candler School of Theology, 1970–90

**P. 73 Roberta Chesnut (Bondi)**
The substance of Roberta Bondi's story is derived from three interviews conducted by Mary Elizabeth Moore on behalf of the Program for Women in Theology and Ministry—October 26, 2005; April 19, 2006; and May 17, 2006—and in a personal interview with the author, May 17, 2013

**P. 75 spring of 1979 Carol Ann Newsom was offered the job**
Personal interview with the author, May 20, 2013

**P. 76 Time—and the appointment of more women at Candler**
Annual reports of the dean, 1978–93

CHAPTER SIX

**P. 83 "We are praying that you will not make a mistake. Signed, the Holy Club"**
Hauk and King, 169–70

**P. 85 Emory College enrollment grew by almost 50 percent and tuition nearly doubled.**
Enrollment data for 1977–78 found in Emory University Annual Administrative Report to the Board of Trustees, November 9, 1978; enrollment data for 1992–93 found in minutes of the Board of Trustees of Emory University, November 11, 1993

**P. 86 served in Mississippi at an important time**
http://www.unitedmethodistreporter
.com/2012/12/um-bishop-mack-b-stokes-dies-at-100/

**P. 87 much of the hard work in preparing for the growth of the 1970s**
Hauk and King, 169

**P. 88 enrollment had climbed from 427 in the fall of 1969 to 588**
Annual Report of the Emory University President to the Board of Trustees, 1968–77

**P. 89 The concept did not always translate easily into practice.**
Luther E. Smith Jr., May 9, 2013, and Robert C. Bondi, May 17, 2013, interviews with author

**P. 89 A second contribution Laney made to the future of Candler**
I owe thanks to David Pacini for making the connection between Laney's sabbatical to Harvard and the later appointments of several faculty members who would play critical roles in Candler's development over the next three decades

**P. 89 the deanship at Harvard might open up for him if he were interested.**
Stuart F. Gulley, *The Academic President as Moral Leader: James T. Laney at Emory University* (Macon, GA: Mercer University Press, 2001), 23

**P. 90 Laney's storied path to and through the Emory presidency**
Gulley, 18–32

CHAPTER SEVEN

This chapter adapts and enlarges upon Gary S. Hauk, "The Pitts Theology Library," in *A Sesquicentennial Chronicle of the Emory University Library*, ed. Thomas H. English, (Atlanta: Friends of the Emory University Libraries, 1987)

**P. 93 twenty-five hundred rare books as well as manuscripts and letters**
Bowen, 24

**P. 95 "the greatest need of our School at the present time"**
Emory University President's Report, 1936–37, 25

**P. 95 "This has been the finest year in the history of the library."**
Quoted in Bowen, 132

**P. 98 what had been their jewel would become their white elephant**
Rhonda Watts, "Antiquarian Quest," *Emory Magazine* (June 1989), 27

**P. 99 disagreement between officials at Hartford and those at Emory**
Correspondence among Jackson W. Carroll, Harvey K. McArthur, Channing R. Jeschke, and Jim L. Waits, June 16, 1977, through October 14, 1977. In annual files of the librarian, Pitts Theology Library archives

**P. 99 Never before in the history of American higher education has a book collection of this size and quality been transferred**
Letter from Channing R. Jeschke to E. Ward King, October 12, 1976. In annual files of the librarian, Pitts Theology Library archives

**P. 99 Pitts would rise to second, before falling behind Union and Princeton.**
Annual Report, Pitts Theology Library, June 30, 1977. Also M. Patrick Graham, email to author, May 16, 2013

**P. 101 The total cost . . . amounted to $3,450,000.**
Annual Report, Pitts Theology Library, June 30, 1978

CHAPTER EIGHT

**P. 108 By 1977, however, nearly 18 percent of Candler's students were women**
Annual report of the Candler School of Theology, 1977

**P. 109 Born of Conviction**
http://www.mississippi-umc.org/console/files/oFiles_Library_XZXLCZ/Born_of_Conviction_4QQJSQYW.pdf

**P. 109 In Nashville he met James Laney**
Jim Waits, personal interview with the author, May 31, 2013

**P. 110 40 percent growth in the student body in only eight years, matched by a 28 percent growth in the faculty**
Annual report of the Candler School of Theology, 1977

**P. 111 stress in the theology school as plans took shape for a new chapel**
Annual Report of the Candler School of Theology, 1978

**P. 115 an altar table whose shape the advisory committee rejected**
Don Saliers, personal interview with the author, April 24, 2013

**P. 116 there simply is no theological faculty in America that rivals them**
Annual Report of the Candler School of Theology, 1979

**P. 116 blending linguistic philosophies, aesthetics, and liturgics**
I am grateful to Brooks Holifield for this insight

**P. 117 questions about the appropriate role of the Black Student Caucus,**
Jim Waits, email to the author, July 29, 2013

**P. 118 each year's series of seminars in CP400**
Mallard Papers (MSS 336).

**P. 121 writing of Wesley in part from a perspective provided by Moltmann**
Once again, thank you, Brooks Holifield

**P. 121 The opening of Cannon Chapel in September 1981**
Annual Report of the Candler School of Theology, 1982

**P. 122 "Rethinking Human Rights"**
"Human Rights," *Daedalus: Journal of the American Academy of Arts and Sciences* (Fall 1983)

**P. 123 the five-year campaign achieved its goal ahead of schedule and closed with $12 million by the end of fiscal year 1988**
Annual Report of the Candler School of Theology, 1988

**P. 125 final meeting with the Candler faculty, in May 1991**
Minutes of the faculty of the Candler School of Theology, May 6, 1991

**P. 126 enrollment in the fall of 1990 had dropped to 455 FTE, down from 490 in 1987; entering MDiv students numbered 101, down from 145 three years earlier**
Annual Report of the Candler School of Theology, 1991

CHAPTER NINE

**P. 131 "the school's mutuality with the church"**
Annual Report of the School of Theology, 1991–92

**P. 131 Dean LaGree announced in August at his first faculty retreat**
Candler School of Theology Faculty Minutes, August 28, 1991

**P. 131 a diminishment of the priority of scholarship in the school**
I am grateful to Brooks Holifield for sharing this bit of faculty perspective

**P. 135 Candler faculty contributed 90 to 95 percent of the teaching and advising to PhD students**
Candler School of Theology Faculty Minutes, August 23, 1993

**P. 136 he retorted that he hoped to be able to do that himself one day**
Steven F. Darsey told me this story about John Haralson Hayes; knowing them both well, I believe it

**P. 136 the percentage of applications accepted fell . . . to 74.1 percent in 1999**
Annual Report of the Candler School of Theology, 1998–99

**P. 136 Some seventeen countries around the world were represented in Candler's student body in 1999**
Annual Report of the Candler School of Theology, 1998–99

**P. 136 development staff raised $600,000 more than it had raised the previous year**
Annual Report of the Candler School of Theology, 1992–93

**P. 137 In the words of its website, YTI "strives to equip young women and men"**
http://www.candler.emory.edu/programs/institutes-initiatives/yti/history.cfm

**P. 137 students had reacted with hostility . . . to the visit of Carter Heyward**
Candler School of Theology Faculty Minutes, November 2, 1992

**P. 139 "unreserved openness in conversation with others"**
John Whitehead, *The Life of the Rev. Charles Wesley* (Boston: Dow and Jackson, 1845), 91

**P. 139 I had one of the most satisfying MTS colloquys**
Hendrikus Boers, letter to Kevin R. LaGree, September 15, 1994, in Papers of Hendrikus Boers (MSS 325), Pitts Theology Library

**P. 143 Candler enrolled one hundred African American students for the first time**
Annual Report of the Candler School of Theology, 1999–2000

CHAPTER TEN

**P. 145 charged a committee in 1988 to look closely at the church's presence at Emory**
Emory University, Committee on the Church's Presence, February 1989

**P. 146 As an agnostic, I simply have seen no evidence of the existence of God.**
William M. Chace, *100 Semesters: My Adventures as Student, Professor, and University President, and What I Learned Along the Way* (Princeton, NJ: Princeton University Press, 2006), 266–67

**P. 149 As two faculty members would later put it, appreciatively**
Carol Newsom, interview with the author, May 20, 2013; Steven Kraftchick, interview with the author, June 3, 2013

**P. 150 Richey would request an explanation from the administration**
Candler School of Theology Faculty Minutes, November 3, 2003

**P. 151 The school thus would have three buildings**
Candler School of Theology Faculty Minutes, October 2, 2000

**P. 151 each year of delay added $1.5 million to projected costs**
Candler School of Theology Faculty Minutes, May 25, 2005

**P. 152 the university would have borne more of the cost of construction**
Steven Kraftchick, interview with the author, June 3, 2013

CHAPTER ELEVEN

**P. 158 Bishop Marshall "Jack" Meadors . . . called her arrival at Candler "providential and exciting"**
"Dean Named at Emory's Candler School of Theology," Emory University news release, May 11, 2006, http://www.emory.edu/news/Releases/CandlerDean1147354693.html

**P. 161 one-third of all the books published by Emory University faculty were published by Candler faculty members**
Candler School of Theology, Annual Report of the Dean, 2009–10

**P. 162 The GPA of the entering class continued to inch upward**
Tables, Candler School of Theology, Annual Report of the Dean, 2011–12

**P. 162 13 million self-identified agnostics and atheists**
http://www.pewforum.org/Unaffiliated/nones-on-the-rise.aspx

**P. 164 compared to 15 percent in 1985**
http://faithandleadership.com/programs/spe/articles/200807/graph_large.jpg

**P. 164 half older, half younger**
http://www.churchleadership.com/research/um_clergy_age_trends08.htm

**P. 165 lost few, if any, to Harvard, Boston, Duke, Yale, or Vandy**
Candler School of Theology Faculty Minutes, April 6, 2009

**P. 165 a reinvigorated Committee of One Hundred**
Candler School of Theology, Annual Report of the Dean, 2009–10

**P. 165 "new economic climate"**
Emory University, Office of the President, 2009 Annual Report, http://www.emory.edu/president/annual-report/ar2009/i-climate.html

**P. 166 the college no longer could pony up $7.5 million**
Candler School of Theology Faculty Minutes, March 2, 2009

**P. 166 Republic of Georgia, Indonesia, and Mozambique**
Candler School of Theology Faculty Minutes, March 2, 2009

**P. 167 needed to find new streams of revenue**
Candler School of Theology Faculty Minutes, May 4, 2009

**P. 167 three hundred applicants each year**
Candler School of Theology Faculty Minutes, November 2, 2009

**P. 168 2012 self-study of the school**
Candler School of Theology, "Self-Study Dean's Narrative," February 2012

CHAPTER TWELVE

**P. 174 Georgia's oldest Maytag washing machine**
Michael C. Carlos Museum, "Introduction," *Michael C. Carlos Museum: Highlights of the Collections* (Atlanta: Emory University, 2011), 5

**P. 178 a student at Emory University published a newspaper editorial**
Ryan Seals, "Emory's Conflicting Missions," *Emory Wheel*, March 23, 2009, http://www.emorywheel.com/archive/detail.php?n=26773

Altizer, Thomas J. J. *Living the Death of God: A Theological Memoir*. New York: State University of New York Press, 2006

———. *Toward a New Christianity: Readings in the Death of God Theology*. New York: Harcourt, Brace and World, 1967

American Academy of Arts and Sciences. *Daedalus: Journal of the American Academy of Arts and Sciences*. Fall 1983

Auslander, Mark. *The Accidental Slaveowner: Revisiting a Myth of Race and Finding an American Family*. Athens: University of Georgia Press, 2011

Beierle, Andrew M. "One Brick from Babylon." *Emory Magazine*, October 1988, 8–18

Boers (Hendrikus E.) Papers (MSS 325). Pitts Theology Library, Emory University

Bondi, Roberta Chesnut. Interviews by Mary Elizabeth Moore on behalf of the Program for Women in Theology and Ministry—October 26, 2005; April 19, 2006; and May 17, 2006—and interview by Gary S. Hauk, May 17, 2013

Bowen, Boone M. *The Candler School of Theology: Sixty Years of Service*. Atlanta: Emory University, 1974

Cannon, William Ragsdale. *A Magnificent Obsession: The Autobiography of William Ragsdale Cannon*. Nashville: Abingdon Press, 1999

Cauthen, Kenneth. *The Impact of American Religious Liberalism*. New York: Harper and Row, 1962

Chace, William M. *100 Semesters: My Adventures as Student, Professor, and University President, and What I Learned Along the Way*. Princeton, NJ: Princeton University Press, 2006

Conklin, Paul K. *Gone with the Ivy: A Biography of Vanderbilt University*. Knoxville: University of Tennessee Press, 1985

Darsey, Steven F. Interview by Gary S. Hauk, May 10, 2013

Day 1. News release. "Historic 'Protestant Hour' Archives to Be Restored." August 2, 2010, http://day1.org/2243-historic_protestant_hour_archives_to_be_restored

Emory University. Board of Trustees. Minutes. Manuscript, Archives, and Rare Book Library (MARBL)

Emory University. Committee on the Church's Presence. February 1989

Emory University. "Dean Named at Emory's Candler School of Theology. News release, May 11, 2006, http://www.emory.edu/news/Releases/CandlerDean1147354693.html

Emory University. *The Emory Alumnus*. MARBL

Emory University. Office of the President. 2009 Annual Report, http://www.emory.edu/president/annual-report/ar2009/i-climate.html

Emory University. President's Reports to the Board of Trustees, 1920–77. MARBL

Emory University, Candler School of Theology. Bulletins of the Candler School of Theology, 1915–2012. MARBL

———. Faculty Minutes, 1971–2010

———. Pitts Theology Library. Annual reports of the librarian. 1975–94

———. "Self-Study Dean's Narrative," February 2012

———. Youth Theological Initiative, http://www.candler.emory.edu/programs/institutes-initiatives/yti/history.cfm

Federal Bureau of Investigation. Memorandum to J. Edgar Hoover. January 29, 1942. http://www.foitimes.com/internment/Arrest01.pdf

Furr, Jerry, et al. "Born of Conviction." *Mississippi Methodist Advocate*, January 2, 1963, http://www.mississippi-umc.org/console/files/oFiles_Library_XZXLCZ/Born_of_Conviction_4QQJSQYW.pdf

Godshalk, David Fort. *Veiled Visions: The 1906 Atlanta Race Riot and the Reshaping of American Race Relations*. Chapel Hill: University of North Carolina Press, 2005

Gulley, Stuart F. *The Academic President as Moral Leader: James T. Laney at Emory University*. Macon, GA: Mercer University Press, 2001

Hahn, Heather M. "UM Bishop Mack B. Stokes Dies at 100." *United Methodist Reporter,* December 10, 2010, http://www.unitedmethodistreporter.com/2012/12/um-bishop-mack-b-stokes-dies-at-100/

Hauk, Gary S. "The Pitts Theology Library." In *A Sesquicentennial Chronicle of the Emory University Library,* ed. Thomas H. English, 33–41. Atlanta: Friends of the Emory University Libraries, 1987

———. and Sally Wolff King, eds. *Where Courageous Inquiry Leads: The Emerging Life of Emory University.* Atlanta: Emory University and Bookhouse Group, 2010

Johnson, Mary Vaughn (Mrs. Emmett). "Job Analysis of a Mother of Preschool Children, as Indicated by Eight Mothers Whose Husbands Were Students in the Candler School of Theology Summer 1936." BD diss., Candler School of Theology, Emory University, 1938. Pitts Theology Library Special Collections

Kean, Melissa F. "'At a Most Uncomfortable Speed': The Desegregation of the South's Private Universities, 1945–1964." PhD diss., Rice University, 2000

Kraftchick, Steven. Interview by Gary S. Hauk. June 3, 2013

Mallard (William) Papers (MSS 336). Pitts Theology Library Archives, Emory University

Marsden, George M. *Fundamentalism and American Culture.* New York: Oxford University Press, 2006

Michael C. Carlos Museum. "Introduction." *Michael C. Carlos Museum: Highlights of the Collections.* Atlanta: Emory University, 2011

Miller, Glenn T. *Piety and Profession: American Protestant Theological Education, 1870–1970.* Grand Rapids: Wm. B. Eerdmans, 2007

Newsom, Carol Ann. Interview by Gary S. Hauk. May 20, 2013

Pacini, David S. Interview by Gary S. Hauk. June 11, 2013

Parker, Franklin N. *What We Believe: Studies in Christian Doctrine.* Nashville: Publishing House of the Methodist Episcopal Church, South, 1924

Pew Research. Religion & Public Life Project. "'Nones' on the Rise." October 9, 2012, http://www.pewforum.org/Unaffiliated/nones-on-the-rise.aspx

Pierce, Alfred M. *Giant Against the Sky: The Life of Bishop Warren Akin Candler.* New York: Abingdon-Cokesbury Press, 1948

Saliers, Don. Interview by Gary S. Hauk. April 24, 2013

Sandeen, Ernest Robert. *The Roots of Fundamentalism: British and American Millenarianism, 1800–1930.* Chicago: University of Chicago Press, 2008

Seals, Ryan. "Emory's Conflicting Missions." *Emory Wheel,* March 23, 2009, http://www.emorywheel.com/archive/detail.php?n=2677

Shelton, William A. *Dust and Ashes of Empires.* Nashville: Cokesbury Press, 1924

Smart, Wyatt Aiken. *The Contemporary Christ: The Fondren Lectures for 1942.* New York: Abingdon-Cokesbury Press, 1942

———. *Still the Bible Speaks.* New York: Abingdon-Cokesbury Press, 1948

———. "They Accused the Bishop of Heresy." *Emory Alumnus* (October 1957): 17–19

Smith, Luther E. Interview by Gary S. Hauk. May 9, 2013

Waits, Jim L. Interview by Gary S. Hauk. May 31, 2013

Watts, Rhonda. "Antiquarian Quest." *Emory Magazine* (June 1989): 25–32

Weems, Lovett H., Jr., and Ann A. Michel. "The Need to Support Young Clergy." Sustaining Pastoral Excellence, Leadership Education at Duke University, 2008, http://faithandleadership.com/programs/spe/articles/200807/youngclergy.html

———. "United Methodist Clergy Age Trends: Why Young Clergy Matter." Lewis Center for Church Leadership, Wesley Theological Seminary, 2008, http://www.churchleadership.com/research/um_clergy_age_trends08.htm

Whitehead, John. *The Life of the Rev. Charles Wesley.* Boston: Dow and Jackson, 1845